KU-063-432

Songs of the *Spirit*

THE PLACE OF PSALMS IN THE WORSHIP OF GOD

EDITED BY

KENNETH STEWART

CHURCH
REPENTANCE & REFORMATION
SCOTLAND

SONGS OF THE SPIRIT

THE PLACE OF PSALMS IN THE WORSHIP OF GOD

Church Repentance & Reformation Scotland

"Lord, I die in the faith that thou wilt not leave Scotland, but that thou wilt make the blood of thy witnesses the seed of thy Church; and return again, and be glorious in our land."
James Renwick (1662-1688), on the scaffold

Copyright © 2014 by Reformation Scotland Trust
except as otherwise indicated.
The copyright in each article is owned by the respective author.
All rights reserved.

First paperback edition printed 2014 in the United Kingdom.

A catalogue record for this book is available from the British Library.

ISBN 978-1-910013-00-7

No part of this book shall be reproduced or transmitted in any form or by any means, electronic or mechanical, including photocopying, recording, or by any information retrieval system without written permission of the publisher.

Published by Reformation Scotland Trust,
Church Office, Muirpark Street, Glasgow G11 5NP.

Designed by Alasdair Macleod.
Cover image © JupiterImages, 2014.

Printed by Bell and Bain Ltd, Glasgow.

We hallow and sanctify God's name when we give Him a holy and spiritual worship.

(1) When we give Him the same kind of worship that He has appointed. 'I will be sanctified in them that come nigh me' (Leviticus 10:3): that is, I will be sanctified with that very worship I have appointed. It is the purity of worship God loves better than the pomp. It dishonours His name to bring anything into His worship which He has not instituted; as if He were not wise enough to appoint the manner in which He will be served. Men prescribe to Him and superadd their inventions; which He looks upon as offering strange fire, and as a high provocation.

(2) When we give to God the same heart devotion in worship He has appointed. 'Fervent in spirit; serving the Lord' (Romans 12:11). The word for fervent is a metaphor, which alludes to water that seethes and boils over; to signify that our affections should boil over in holy duties. To give God outside worship, and not the devotion of the heart, instead of hallowing and sanctifying Him in an ordinance, is to abuse Him; as if one calls for wine and you give him an empty glass. It is to deal with God as Prometheus did with Jupiter, who did eat the flesh and present Jupiter with nothing but bones covered over with skin. We hallow God's name and sanctify Him in an ordinance when we give Him the vitals of religion, and a heart flaming with zeal.

Thomas Watson – *The Lord's Prayer* (1692)

Songs of the Spirit

TABLE OF CONTENTS

Preface - *Donald Macdonald*   **9**

Introduction - *Kenneth Stewart*   **15**

I. What Shall We Sing in the Worship of God?   **17**
Kenneth Stewart

II. The Singing of Psalms in the Worship of God   **55**
William Maclean

III. Christ in All the Psalms   **71**
Donald Balfour

IV. The Praise of the Sanctuary   **77**
William Mackay

V. Sing the Lord's Song   **91**
John Keddie

VI. Therapeutic Praise   **147**
David Murray

VII. Is the Psalter Enough?   **151**
David Silversides

VIII. Christ's Abiding Presence in the Psalms   **169**
Matthew Vogan

IX. What Should Accompany Our Worship of God?   **175**
Kenneth Stewart

Appendix - Minority Report on Public Worship   **195**
John Murray & William Young

Preface

Donald Macdonald

Call upon me in the day of trouble:
I will deliver thee, and thou shalt glorify me.
(Psalm 50:15)

When I first thought of sponsoring the printing and distribution of this collection of articles on the use of the Psalms in worship, I remembered a number of Christian believers I have known over the years who expressed their appreciation for the Psalms and particularly the Scottish Psalter, which they had the privilege of memorising in childhood. Some have commented to me that when the mind wanders in prayer, they re-focus by quoting the familiar words of the Psalter. I particularly remember once visiting a lady in hospital who had to lie flat. She related to me how she valued being able to recite the Metrical Psalms as a prayer, since her illness was so severe that she was unable to form a coherent prayer of her own, but could still pray in the words of the Psalms, secure in her memory through long years of use.

Indeed, this is a thoroughly Scriptural experience, as one of the clearest examples of prayer in the Bible is that of Jonah from the whale's belly, recorded in Jonah 2, where, over just eight verses, he includes no less than twelve quotations or parallels from the Book of Psalms. Since hearing of these experiences, I have meditated on and hence valued the prayerful content of the Psalms, especially as they express both human experience and needs which were no different in the Psalmists' days than they are in ours. God is also the same God.

It was Thomas Watson who said: 'Prayer is our chief duty and brings Heaven down to man. There is no duty that has so many promises attached to it, albeit most of them conditional. It gives more honour to God and brings more blessings from God.' Bernard called prayer 'the conqueror of Him who is invincible,' and Luther said it was 'omnipotent'. I admire these words of John Bunyan on this subject:

> Prayer brings those who have the spirit of supplication into great familiarity with God. Those who pray receive great things for themselves and for those they pray for. Prayer opens the heart of God and fills the empty soul. By prayer, the Christian can open his heart to God as to a friend, and obtain fresh testimony of God's friendship to him... True prayer feels, sighs, groans, and bubbles out of the heart as some heavy burden lies upon it or some sweet sense of mercy received is appreciated. O the heat, strength, life, vigour and affection that is in true prayer!

No one can deprive a believer of this privilege, and the Psalms are there to help us! In practice they will be found much easier to commit to memory in metrical form, especially the classic versions found in the *Scottish Psalter* of 1650. This collection is part of our spiritual, national and Reformation heritage and does not deserve a subordinate position in public worship, any more than it held for the generations that went before us.

Today, the Christian Church in Scotland, heir to this glorious heritage, is painfully and tragically divided. I value the wisdom of J C Ryle on this subject: 'The divisions of Christians are one great cause of the weakness of the visible church. They often absorb energy, time, and power, which might have been well bestowed on better things. They furnish the infidel with a prime argument against the truth of Christianity. They help the devil. Satan indeed is the chief promoter of religious divisions. If he cannot extinguish Christianity, he labours to make Christians quarrel with one another, and to set every man's hand against his neighbour. None knows better than the devil, that "to divide is to conquer"' (*Expository Thoughts on Mark*, 1985, pp.54-55). I recently challenged a devout, highly respected and experienced Free Presbyterian Minister on the curse of denominations, to which he answered that denominations were abominations to the Lord.

It is worth remembering that before the time of these divisions the Reformed Church in Scotland used the Psalms as the exclusive method of praise, and that was accompanied by much spiritual prosperity for our nation. There is an undeniable connection between spiritual and national prosperity, and perhaps the lack of the latter at present has something to do with our failure to seek earnestly for the glory of God in Scotland.

Since I began reflecting on these things, I heard a challenging sermon on the subject 'What kind of worship should we give to God, that which man chooses or that which God Himself has commanded?' This question really sums up the whole thrust of this book. Not only does it challenge the individual and eternal responsibility all believers have, particularly Church leaders of all denominations, it also left me in no doubt that this publication is both desirable and necessary to promote repentance and reformation within today's Christian Church.

In no area are the worship trends of today more obviously man-centred than in the content of the sung praise of God. This whole tendency is aptly critiqued by the Christian writer Warren

Wiersbe: 'Many individual believers and entire congregations have imitated Abraham and 'run to Egypt' to get help. They stop being outsiders; they lose their separation from the world and start promoting imitation of the world. Sanctuaries become theatres, worship leaders become entertainers and everybody is happy except the Lord. The Word of God and prayer are minimized, booming music is maximized and the gospel is merchandised. This may be one way to build a crowd, but is it God's way to glorify Jesus Christ and build a church? Consider what Paul wrote in First Thessalonians 2: 1-7 and take it to heart.' (*Too Soon to Quit*, 2010, p.20).

It is to try to provide help in this area, to churches and pastors alike, that I have encouraged the publication of this book. The eight chapters included in the collection together build a powerful argument towards one firm conclusion: that God has commanded that he be praised in the words of the Divinely-inspired Psalms, and that these Psalms are entirely sufficient for worship.

I am and have personally been blessed to experience sound gospel teaching over many decades and yet the chapters of this book, as I read them, exposed more spiritual ignorance in my heart than I could have suspected. I realised that I had never fully appreciated the importance of singing Psalms in public worship as opposed to hymns of human composition in public worship. I was oblivious to the gulf of difference between the two, and the seriousness of the choice that must be made. Yet as I researched the whole subject of church praise, it became clear to me that my personal ignorance was not isolated, but may well be prevalent among my peer group, and to an even greater extent among the generations coming after me.

As I meditate and ponder on the solemnity of this publication as it relates to the question, 'Do we worship God according to his will and pleasure or according to our own human motivation?' I pray, particularly for worship and church leaders, who are the most privileged but also the most responsible section of society to be challenged by the question. The consequences of my leadership, good or bad, will finish with my retirement or death, whichever the Lord deems appropriate, but the responsibility of every worship and church leader's spiritual depth is, for themselves and for their followers, infinitely and eternally and seriously consequential. It is solemn food for thought, meditation and indeed deserves commitment to prayer.

It is my firm conviction that the only standard that matters is how our final Judge measures each one of us, including how we worship Him. I hope that as you read this book you will be challenged to consider that the worship that God accepts is that which he has appointed, not that which man chooses. That principle is equally true for the reformation of the Christian Church, and although I accept that that is a deeper and wider subject, the restoration of Psalm singing in public worship is undoubtedly one aspect of such necessary reformation.

As with any task that I set myself, or that has been set for me, I began to seek Divine guidance on the whole matter. After some weeks, the needed inspiration came from the fourth Chapter of Hebrews in the first three verses:
'Let us therefore fear, lest, a promise being left us of entering into His rest, any of you should seem to come short of it. For unto us was the gospel preached, as well as unto them: but the word preached did not profit them, not being mixed with faith in them that heard it. For we which have believed do enter into rest, as he said, As I have sworn in my wrath, if they shall enter into my rest.'

The three words contained within these verses which resonated with me were 'fear', 'short' of a promise (and could it be that by not using the Psalms we are falling short of a promise?), and the 'wrath' of God. The fear of the Lord is a subject rarely discussed in most church circles, even from the pulpit. The wrath of God is taboo. The truth of this was sadly vindicated to me at a recent funeral where Psalm 90 was read as the 'lesson', but the two verses containing 'wrath' and 'anger' were deliberately left out of the reading of the Psalm.

Since then, I have spoken collectively and individually to a number of evangelical pastors regarding the link between the 'old paths' (as recommended to us in Jeremiah 6:16), Psalm singing in worship and the reformation of the Church. Individually, without exception, all agreed on the need for reformation in worship but equally, when it came to the specifics of implementing this, all differed. Reformation had to be on their individual, and sadly varied, terms; and this only reflected their varying personal, spiritual and doctrinal values.

Before parting from each of these amicable meetings, I asked the pastors individually how the gap between their perception of reformation and God's standard could be bridged, given that He does not compromise. That question was a conversation stopper! It was interesting that these same Church leaders told me that, as a group, they could not agree on a way forward since they could not unite around a single foundation of practise in worship, and particularly in praise. It was painfully evident, even to a layman, that the variety in worship practised by the congregations represented had only led to confusion as to what the Church should actually teach.

Therefore, let us be guided by the teaching of Scripture, in this area as in all others: 'Stand in the ways and see, and ask for the old paths, where the good way is, and walk in it; then you will find rest for your souls' (Jeremiah 6:16).

Introduction

Kenneth Stewart

Issues concerning the theology and practice of worship have become increasingly problematic in the life of the Christian church. This has been the case for some time but especially so since the growth of more distinctively charismatic forms of worship from the mid-twentieth century onwards.

This charismatic emphasis has led to an increasing impetus for change in the more mainstream churches and the Presbyterian churches of Scotland are no exception – so much so that it is now becoming increasingly rare to find churches which practice the singing of hymns to the accompaniment of a single musical instrument such as a piano or an organ.

In the midst of such evolution, it is easily forgotten that the original Presbyterian form of worship had no room for hymns or instruments at all! For the original Presbyterians, the singing of God's praise meant the singing of Psalms without musical accompaniment. Notably, with the exception of the Lutherans, this was also the practice of the churches of the Magisterial Reformation within the British Isles and on the continent. Furthermore, however surprising it may seem, they adopted this practice on the ground of biblical conviction rather than expediency, claiming that it was a return to *apostolic* as well as *historic* worship.

The decline of Presbyterian Scotland is a matter often discussed but the role played in that decline by alterations to the worship of the church is seldom mentioned if at all. However, God is a jealous God and if the singing of Psalms without the accompaniment of musical instruments is indeed the correct way for the church to approach God in worship and if this nation has been privileged enough to know that truth and enjoy its benefits, then it should not be a surprise if the abandonment of it has been a cause of God's displeasure against the church and the nation.

The only way to go forward is to go back. The answer to the widespread confusion and apostasy lies in the recovery of truths once heartily embraced – and, indeed, sworn to – but now largely abandoned and forgotten. It is the conviction of all who contribute to this book that the recovery of earnest, intelligent and spiritual unaccompanied singing of Psalms in the praise of the church is a major part of the repentance and renewal so badly needed in the church today.

Of course, more is needed for repentance than that. And more needs to be said on worship itself than this. However, this issue needs to be addressed before unaccompanied Psalm singing disappears – in what would be another of God's judgements upon our land.

I.

What Should We Sing in the Worship of God?
An Argument from Scripture for Exclusive Psalm Singing

Kenneth Stewart

INTRODUCTION

M ost church-going people will be aware of significant changes in worship content and style over recent years – particularly in connection with the songs offered to God as part of that worship.

Of course, it is natural for mankind to compose and to sing and it is no less natural for redeemed mankind to compose and to sing in praise of God. What is surprising, however, is the extraordinary rise in the number of Christian songs being written and performed since the second half of the 20th century. No less surprising is the ease with which so many of these songs have found their way into the worship of the church.

In an area where many are, for several reasons, instinctively conservative, this development has provoked quite a reaction – on grounds both of principle and taste. However, those in favour of the development generally dismiss this reaction as 'traditionalism' - and, to be fair, they do have a point: after all, it is simply not true to say – as so many do – that the old songs are always better. Sometimes they are but sometimes they are not. In any case, it is hard to see how the mere fact of having been around for a long time entitles a worship song to hold its place forever against a newer rival of superior quality.

However, most people fail to address the deeper questions – and that is the case whether they are for the change or not. These questions concern the criteria we should be applying when it comes to choosing which songs we should use in the worship of God in the first place. For example, consider the following questions:

'Who should write the worship songs of the church? Who should decide their suitability for use? Who should decide which songs should be sung on any occasion? Is it acceptable for an unbeliever to write a worship song if the song expresses the truth? Does a song have to mention God or Jesus explicitly before it can be accepted for use in worship? Would it be acceptable for a song just to contain truth in general or would it have to contain expressly theological truth in order to be considered for use in worship? Does a worship song need to address God directly?

Have you ever thoughts of these questions? How confident would you be in answering questions of this kind? Would you even know where to begin in trying to answer them? The chances are that most people have never considered these questions seriously enough – if at all.

The purpose of this chapter is to present a case for using only the Psalms of the Bible when we offer our singing to God in worship – and that we should sing these Psalms without the accompaniment of musical instruments.

If your instinctive response to this argument is to see it as novel or bizarre, it may come as something of a shock to you to discover that this way of singing to God in worship was once the accepted norm in the Reformed Churches of Europe! In fact, the mighty movement of God in the 16th century – known as the Reformation – saw the establishment of the regular congregational worship of God, in almost all the Reformed churches, precisely along these lines! And this was no accident: The Reformation was not just a reformation of *doctrine* and *church government* but a reformation of *worship* as well. In the movement of Reformation, the authority of scripture was of paramount importance and this guiding principle determined the content and form of worship as well as the doctrine of the church and its government. And for John Calvin – and indeed for most of the other leading 16th century Reformers – the Bible only authorised the singing of Psalms alone without instrumental accompaniment.

> "The overwhelming majority of Reformed churches in Europe adopted the practice of unaccompanied psalm singing in their worship"

It is hardly surprising, then, that the large family of Reformed churches which were distinguished from others by use of Calvin's name (Calvinist) – and which made up the overwhelming majority of Reformed churches in Europe – adopted the practice of unaccompanied psalm singing in their worship.

Significantly, although they did stress that this was the practice of the church in the days immediately following the Apostles (see further below), their main reason for adopting this position was that they understood it to be the Biblical position on worship. And this is the conviction behind this chapter too – the conviction that God has given us a book of songs for singing and that we are obligated to sing these songs and to sing them exclusively in the worship of his name.

Sadly, however, over the last 150 years, this form of worship has become increasingly rare. Over recent years in particular, as we noted above, Reformed worship has changed almost beyond recognition and is now often dominated by songs of merely human composition and by instrumental musical performance.

To examine how, when and why all this changed would take too long and lies beyond our scope. My primary concern here is to defend this historic position and to promote it as the form of worship which God requires and which, therefore, most glorifies him and tends most to our spiritual health and edification.

To help you see where I'm coming from, it's important to state at the outset that I am writing from the standpoint of someone who believes that every part of worship (such as singing, prayer, preaching or reading) needs a *clear commandment of God to authorise it*. In other words, when it comes to worship, it is never enough to say 'God *doesn't condemn it so it must be alright to do it*'. Instead, we must be able to say 'God *commands this to be done and therefore I must do it*'. I will say something more on this as we go on.

Where, then, do we begin?

Perhaps it makes sense to begin with the following question: If unaccompanied psalm singing was the norm in the Calvinistic churches of Europe following the Reformation, what were the arguments used to move these churches in another direction?

When we address this question, we discover that the arguments used at that time to stimulate this change are the same arguments being used now to further it! We also discover that, however many forms these arguments seem to take, they seem to reduce down, in essence, to two – first, the Bible commands this change and, second, the events of the New Testament necessitate it!

Interestingly, these two arguments appeared recently (2010) in a paper specially written to defend the use of new songs, and of instrumental accompaniment, in the worship of the New Testament church. As I go on, I will make some references to this paper – just to clarify the arguments. The paper is entitled *Biblical Interpretation: Music and Song in Worship*, by Rev. A. I. Macleod,

and the full text may be consulted online at URL: http://www.
freechurch.org/images/uploads/Biblical_Interpretation_-_
Music_and_Song_in_Worship_-_A_I_Macleod.pdf.

In what follows, then, we will examine these two arguments
for change in some detail. The issue of instrumental music will be
dealt with in a separate chapter.

TWO ARGUMENTS FOR CHANGE

'Sing a New Song!'
The first argument for using songs other than the Psalms is that
the Bible tells us to do so – therefore, we should sing them!

Now, it is indeed true that the Bible does command us to
sing 'new' songs. We see such a command, for example, in Psalms
33:3; 96:1 and 98:1. Also, some people argue that we have examples
of such new songs in the New Testament book of Revelation.

In the same way, it is argued that the presence of other
'scripture songs' in the Bible is evidence of the on-going composing
and singing of 'new songs' in the worship of the church as and when
such songs were needed – these songs, of course, are additional
to the ones which were later recorded for our use in the Book of
Psalms.

Those who advocate this position, then, are not just
asserting that we should sing these scripture songs themselves
but that we should see their very presence as an indicator that we
should be engaged in a constant process of writing and singing
such songs for use in the worship of the church.

So then, the first argument asserts that the Bible commands
the on-going composition of new worship songs.

'The Psalms are no longer sufficient'
The second argument for adding to the Psalms is a more familiar
one: it is the argument that the Book of Psalms – as a book written
during the time of the Old Covenant – is simply insufficient for
the praise of the church under the New Covenant.

"Are the 'heavenly' songs recorded in the Bible for our use in singing the Songs of the Lord here on earth or are they recorded for some other purpose?"

I think it is important to note that this argument is the oldest, the most emotive (*'Why can't we sing the name of Jesus?'*) and the most powerful argument for the development of hymnody. Indeed, as a simple matter of fact, it has been the most effective argument in the process of first supplementing and then gradually replacing the Psalms as the songbook of the Reformed Churches during the last 150 years.

Of course, these arguments have been well answered before. But it is important to keep answering them whenever they appear and what follows below is designed to do just that.

First, then, we need to examine what the Bible means by singing new songs.

I. 'SING A NEW SONG!'

When it comes to the command to sing new songs, we need to begin by finding out what these new songs are – as opposed to what we think they are!

For this, it is probably best to begin at the end – with the book of Revelation! After all, although the command to sing new songs is a command which appears in the Book of Psalms, most people are unaware of this command and are perhaps more familiar with the singing of new songs in the only place where we find them explicitly sung: the Book of Revelation. These new songs appear in Revelation 5:9-14, 14:3 and 15:3-4.

But what do these passages really teach?

The Songs of Revelation

When we study these songs, one thing is immediately apparent: all of them are being sung in heaven! This should prompt a question: are these 'heavenly' songs recorded in the Bible for our use in singing the Songs of the Lord here on earth or are they recorded for some other purpose? It is probably best to examine them in turn.

Revelation 5:9-14

The song most often appealed to in this debate is found in Revelation 5:9-14. This passage contains a 'new song' declaring the worthiness of the Lamb, praising him as the Redeemer of his people and ascribing honour, glory and power to him.

The writer of the paper I referred to earlier wonders why anyone should be prohibited from singing these words in a services of worship and, in a passionate plea for the worship of heaven to be copied in the worship of the church on earth, he closes his paper by asking a question which, for him, and probably for others, sums up the whole issue:

> *"We too are called to sing, 'Worthy is the Lamb!' At the end of this paper, if anyone is looking for one issue that can absolutely focus the discussion, I offer this question: 'Can we sing, "Worthy is the Lamb!" in public worship?' If not, please tell me why not."*

On first reading, all this may seem convincing enough. However, the argument doesn't bear close scrutiny. Is it really as obvious as he claims it to be that the worship of heaven should be copied by us here on earth? Let us take a moment to follow such an idea through.

If you look more closely at the passage, you will see that the particular song he highlights is being sung in heaven by the 'living creatures' and by the 'twenty-four elders' around the throne. You will see also that while they sing, they all carry a harp and a vessel with incense which contains the prayers of the saints. Another new song (if that is what it is) in Revelation 7:10-12, is sung while waving palm branches and wearing white robes.

Now, if the singing of these new songs in the worship of

heaven is our warrant for singing them right now in our worship on earth, then it would seem fairly obvious that it is also a warrant for singing them with the harp, the incense vessels, the branches and the robes! If, as the writer insists, this singing should be done *as it is done in heaven* then all of these are as much part of the worship as the words which are sung!

Indeed, on the principle of Bible interpretation being applied by the writer, *all the liturgical acts accompanying the offering of heavenly praise in Revelation should all be offered on earth too!* Now, I have seen this kind of thinking argued energetically before – most recently in Lutheran Reconstructionism – but I am surprised to see it in masquerading as classic Presbyterianism.

However, if heaven's worship is to be copied on earth then it is to be copied. Selective applications will not do.

Revelation 14:3

The 'new song' of Revelation 14:3 is even more problematic. Look closely and you will see that this is a song which *no-one can sing at all* – except the 144,000 who are redeemed from the earth! What sense does it make to assert that we should be singing a song which *no-one can sing at all* – except the 144,000 who are redeemed from the earth!

Indeed, this particular example takes us rather neatly to the whole point at issue: all of these songs are clearly sung by angels and glorified saints and they provide glimpses of what is taking place in heaven. By what reasoning, then, should we conclude that these performances by the *church triumphant* in heaven are a mandate for the worship of the *church militant* here on the earth? Is it not far more natural to conclude that what we have in these new songs are heavenly scenes which are simply not meant to be copied on the earth at all?

All this is further highlighted when we ask a more fundamental question: In what way are these songs *'new'*? And, here, it is really easy to be led astray by a false assumption regarding these 'new' songs. The false assumption is that the *'newness'* of these songs must consist in their being '*new covenant*' songs and that they were written to be sung by us in our new covenant worship.

But is this really the case? No, it is not. In point of fact, the 'newness' of these songs is not a reference to these songs being '*New Covenant*' songs but as being songs belonging to the *new order of things in the final state*!

To see this more plainly, just stop to think of the other '*new things*' which appear in the book of Revelation: there is a '*new Jerusalem*' (3:12,21:2), there is a '*new heaven and a new earth*'(21:2), there is a '*new name*' given to God's people (2:17,3:12) and, finally, we have '*all things new*' (21:5). What do all these things have in common? They all they all belong explicitly to *heaven* or to the '*final state*'! The 'newness' of all of these things belongs to the future – to those who have 'overcome' (2:17). That is not true of us yet on the earth!

Again, it is worthwhile noting that all of these 'new' things are of immediate Divine origin. None of them are made by man: It is God who makes the '*new creature*', it is God who makes the '*new cosmos*', it is God who gives the '*new name*' and it is God who inspires the '*new song*' – and they all belong to heaven. In other words, we have no more warrant to make a new song then we do to give ourselves a new name! Both are God's prerogative. I will say more on this below.

Clearly, then, these new songs in Revelation are not designed to form part of the content of our praise book here below. We are given these words simply as comforting insights into the praise of the church as it has overcome above and as a foretaste of a new order of things to be – but the worship performance of these songs awaits the pilgrim people of God in heaven.

For now, God wills that we use the songbook of the church *militant*, not that of the church *triumphant*.

So then, the presence of new songs in the book of Revelation has nothing to say to us in connection with which worship songs should be used here on earth.

Other 'new songs' in the New Testament

What, then, about the other 'songs' which appear in the New Testament?

It may come as something of a surprise to you to discover that there are no such 'songs' in the New Testament at all! Significantly, apart from the Book of Revelation, and its insights into heaven, no other New Testament book speaks about singing new songs.

Unfortunately, that hasn't stopped those who wish to sing them from trying to find them! In fact, it has been alleged for years that we have fragments of such 'new songs' in Philippians 2:5-11, 1 Timothy 3:16 and elsewhere.

Frankly, it is always disappointing to find advocates of hymnody appealing to the alleged presence of so-called 'Apostolic hymn fragments' in the New Testament. If these 'fragments' are anything more than exalted prose they could just as easily be fragments of early creeds. But the stubborn fact remains that, despite the ingenuity of scholars determined to identify such fragments, there is simply no real evidence for their existence. The fragments cannot be proven to be fragments and the hymns from which the 'fragments' came have never been found.

The significance of this failure cannot be overstated: hymnody is an *enduring art form* and, this being so, the utter absence of hymns from the first 200 years (and more) of post-Apostolic church history is a huge problem for those who believe that they were sung throughout the churches by the Apostles and by their successors. Indeed, their absence is as much of a problem for the advocates of hymnody as the absence of musical instruments in the first 800 years of church history is for the advocates of instrumental music (see below).

This is particularly the case if these 'hymns' were so important as to be partly incorporated into the New Testament letters. After all, the argument for their existence is based on supposed fragments appearing in these letters. However, if they really did exist and if they were known and memorised by the Apostles, sung regularly in their worship and incorporated into their letters, their disappearance from the record of history becomes simply and utterly inexplicable.

Indeed, the fact of their apparent 'disappearance' becomes almost conclusive evidence against their alleged existence in the first place!

In this connection, it may surprise most readers to discover that the only religious song

"The original introduction of extra-biblical songs into the worship of the church appears to have been the work of the heretics and not of the orthodox"

surviving from this period is Clement of Alexandria's *Hymn to the Divine Logos* – which is not of good quality and which was probably not designed to be used in public worship. Indeed, there is no evidence that it was ever so used.

In fact, the original introduction of extra-biblical songs into the worship of the church appears to have been the work of the heretics and not of the orthodox. Arius used the writing of songs of praise as a vehicle to spread his false teaching while, according to Eusebius the historian, Paul of Samosata substituted new songs in place of the 'psalms (which are) in honour of our Lord Jesus Christ'. Also, and as late as 430 AD, Augustine – who, in spite of assertions to the contrary, never advocated the use of hymns – could say that the Donatists reproached the church for using Divine songs while they 'were inflaming their minds by singing songs of human composition'.

Without digressing too much into the history of sung praise, it is worth noting that even when such songs began to be used in the churches, the opposition to them was strong: as late as 343 AD, the Council of Laodicea forbad the 'singing of uninspired hymns in church' as well as the 'reading of the uncanonical books of scripture' – a finding which was ratified by the famous Council of Chalcedon. Incidentally, it is important to note the logic applied by the Council – to read a book of human composition, however good it may be, in place of scripture in worship is the same kind of error as to sing a song of human composition in place of scripture in the same act of worship!

However, the purpose of all this is just to show that the attempt to find fragments of hymns in the New Testament literature is futile. The attempt to identify them has long since become an exercise in *scholastic speculation* - the kind of speculation indulged in by academics who have given up the study of what is revealed in exchange for the pursuit of novelty and spurious originality – not to mention academic degrees!

In the face of an utter lack of evidence for their existence, the quest to find them should simply be given up - they are less likely to be found than Atlantis or the Abominable Snowman. In point of fact, in this kind of debate, there should be no appeal to these so-called fragments anymore and the appearance of any such appeal must be interpreted as an admission of weakness in the argument on the part of those who make it.

'Psalms, Hymns and Spiritual Songs' – are they new songs?
Aside from the specific command to sing new songs, the most common argument for their use is found in Paul's command to the churches in Ephesus and Colossae to sing *'psalms, hymns and spiritual songs'*(Ephesians 5:18 and Colossians 3:16).

Admittedly, these are the only passage of scripture which can be appealed to as giving some express warrant to sing something other than the Psalms. And of course, such express warrant is important when it comes to a truly Reformed theology of worship. However, it is important to come to a command like this in a fresh way and, particularly, to see it through first century eyes rather than twenty first century ones! In other words, we shouldn't begin by asking what these words mean to us but what they meant, first of all, to those who wrote them and those who heard them.

When we do this, we discover something interesting: most of the Psalms in the Book of Psalms contain either one or more of the terms *'psalm', 'hymn'* and *'song'* in their titles! In 67 of these psalms, the word *'psalm'* appears in the title. In six of them, the word *'hymn'* appears while in another 35, the word *'song'* appears. Significantly, some of the psalms carry two of these titles together (for example, Psalm 65 is *'a psalm* and *song* of David') while one psalm carries all three titles: Psalm 76 in the Greek translation – which the Apostles used and were familiar with – is a *'psalm'*, a *hymn* and a *'song'*! These titles themselves would be simply the Greek translation of the three Hebrew words used in these Psalm titles: 'Mizmorim' (Psalms), 'Tehillim' (Hymns) and 'Shirim' (Songs).

In proper historical context, then, the presumption would be that Paul is referring to these titles from the Book of Psalms – indeed, that he is referring to the Book of Psalms itself. This becomes all the more plain when we consider some aspects of the translation and interpretation of the passage concerned.

It is significant that a legitimate translation of the Greek passage under discussion would read like this: *'psalms, hymns and songs – spiritual'*. In other words, the adjective 'spiritual' could well be qualifying all three nouns. The significance of this lies in the fact that the word 'spiritual' appears 25 times in the New Testament: On 24 of these occasions, it is a reference to what is produced by the Holy Spirit of God – the only exception to this rule is the reference to 'spiritual wickedness' in Ephesians 6 – which is a reference to what is produced by the spirits of the demonic world. This being the case, the term would seem to be referring here to psalms, hymns and songs which have been *authored for use by the Holy Spirit himself through the process of inspiration*. If this is indeed the best translation, it would only serve to make Paul's reference here to the Book of Psalms even more explicit.

In fairness, however, it could well be the case that the adjective 'spiritual' is merely describing the last of these nouns so

> "As far as the Bible itself is concerned, the evidence points to the three terms as referring to the same body of songs – the Book of Psalms!"

that the meaning would be *'psalms, hymns and spiritual songs'.* However, this does not affect the argument as much as one would think. After all, if these 'songs' are to be 'spiritual' – that is, inspired by the Spirit of God – why should it be the case that they alone are to be inspired while the 'psalms' and the 'hymns' could be uninspired? If, rather, the point is being made that the praise of the church must be inspired by the Holy Spirit, then the attaching of the adjective to 'songs' alone would be on the assumption that the Psalms and hymns were understood to be inspired anyway and would be serving to draw attention to the nature of the Christian's song - when filled with the Holy Spirit – as opposed to those who sing when they are 'filled with wine.'

In other words, the meaning of the passage concerned would be as follows: 'Don't let your speech be the effusions of those who are full of wine, rather let it be the effusions of those who are filled with the Holy Spirit of God – and let your joyful singing not be the production of wine either but rather let it be the joyful singing of those who sing the songs the Holy Spirit himself has given.'

In context, then, it makes no real sense to interpret these terms in the way in which most people carelessly interpret them: the contemporary tendency to use the term *'psalms'* for the songs of the Old Testament and the terms *'hymns'* and *'songs'* for our own compositions has no support in scripture at all. As far as the Bible itself is concerned, the evidence points to the three terms as referring to the same body of songs – the Book of Psalms!

And, again in context, such a reference to well-known songs is only to be expected: After all, these psalms were the songs known and learned by the apostles - and indeed by Christ – and from which they proved the Divinity of Christ (see especially the early chapters of Acts and Hebrews) and in which they saw his person and work most clearly demonstrated. Every instance of Apostolic singing in the New Testament, as we shall see, is best understood as a singing of the psalms, hymns and spiritual songs which were familiar to them but which had now become 'new' in the light of the resurrection of Christ.

Sadly, this understanding of the text has been dismissed, sometimes in a rather cavalier fashion, by more recent interpreters as a case of 'special pleading'. However, it was a commonly held opinion in exegetical texts of the past, is held by many still and remains – in context – the most natural meaning of the text. This interpretation is also strengthened by the way in which the three terms are used interchangeably in reference to the Book of Psalms by such ancient writers as Clement of Alexandria, Philo, Josephus and Athanasius. Indeed, Athanasius, in his celebrated letter to Marcellinus regarding the singing of Psalms, refers to the Psalms of the Bible by the three Greek terms under discussion within the space of a few paragraphs!

As for the various shades of meaning intended to be conveyed by the three terms, I think that a conclusive answer is elusive – but this shouldn't be surprising. After all, the Bible contains several instances of a single body of work, or a unit of some kind, being referred to by three distinct terms which are not always easy to distinguish. For example, in what is a clear reference to the body of 'law' given by God, what are the exact distinctions between *commandments, statutes and judgements* (Deuteronomy 30:16)? Or, in what is a clear reference to the entity of 'sin', what are the exact distinctions between *iniquity, transgression and sin* (Exodus 34:7)? Finally, in what is a clear reference to miracles, what are the exact distinctions between *signs, wonders and miracles* (2 Corinthians 12:12)?

Finding these shades of meaning has its own importance – but is not crucial to the argument: after all, it is simply a fact that the three terms concerned are used as headings – either on their own or in combination – in the Book of Psalms and, at this level, that is all we need to know.

When all this is said and done, it may be useful to highlight that none of this is meant to discourage the writing or singing of songs which are in praise of God. Many such songs – for example, 'When I Survey the Wondrous Cross' – have found their way into the affections of many of the Lord's people and, providing the content is honouring to God, the writing of such songs and their performance can be seen as the valid exercise of a valid gift. However, the questions at issue concern *when*, *where* and *how* such songs are to be used.

After all, it is the Reformed understanding of worship that worship takes place when we draw near to God by calling upon his name. This worship consists of an act, or a series of acts, in which God speaks to us (in reading, preaching and sacraments) and in which we present our offerings to God (in song and prayer – sometimes accompanied with vows and fasting). It is also the historic Reformed understanding that nothing is to be offered to God *as worship* without his explicit appointment – and that the songs which he has appointed to be offered in the context of worship are the Psalms!

This should alert us to the problem involved in binding up these merely human songs along with the Psalms in one volume of praise. And the problem is deeper than we realise. It is not simply a question of how many of God's songs we sing and how many we sing of our own. Certainly, there is a problem there: after all, what does it say about the relative value and authority of God's songs and ours if we choose to sing one of God's in worship and three of our own? But the problem is deeper than that: when a congregation is assembling to offer its tribute of praise to God, what authority do we have for binding Divine and human songs together in that praise offering as though they are of equal value and authority in the praise of God? Would we seriously consider binding up the sermons of John Piper, or even the Apocrypha, with the canonical books of the Bible for public reading? I assume we would not. In the same way, then, we should not be binding up human songs along with Divine songs for public praise.

Please note that this is not an issue of what we bind together *as such* – after all, the Westminster Shorter Catechism was often bound with the multiplication table! It is rather a question of what is of proper Divine authority and use. It appears obvious to me that, in all that is being done in connection with worship, the issues are simply not being thought through.

I suppose all this touches on a related issue – what does God appear to bless? For example, if God uses a hymn to move a soul in his worship, does this not sanction the use of the hymns in singing God's praise? Well, if it does, it would also sanction the reading of the Apocrypha if a reading from it was used to move a soul in the same way! However, as Reformed Christians, we must decide for once and for all whether principles and practice are to be governed by the word of God or by human experience.

The fact is that, in the worship of God, a good song of our composing cannot replace a psalm for the singing any more than a good book of our composing can replace the Bible for reading!

Bearing in mind, then, that the introduction of any form of worship needs explicit authorisation from the word of God – in other words, it is not enough to argue that it is not *forbidden*: it has to be shown to be *commanded* – even the most passionate advocates of hymnody would have to acknowledge that the case for singing uninspired songs is not proven on the basis of the command to praise God in *'psalms, hymns and spiritual songs'*.

What, then, about the other songs which appear in the Old Testament?

Other 'new songs' in the Old Testament
As we saw earlier, there is indeed a clear command to sing new songs in the Old Testament. We find it repeatedly in Psalms 33:3,

40:3, 96:1, 98:1, 144:9 and 149:1. Is this command authorising or indeed commanding us, to write and sing our own worship songs? Again, we need to begin by asking what these songs are!

First, it is important to note that what these psalms actually command us to do is to '*sing*' new songs – not to '*write*' them! This may appear to be an insignificant distinction – after all, how are we to sing one unless we write it first! – but the distinction is not insignificant at all. On the few occasions on which this command is given, the most natural understanding of it is to see it as a reference to the singing of *that particular song itself*. In other words, the psalm which tells us to sing a new song *is itself* the new song!

Probably the most plain example of this is Psalm 40:3, which David describes as a 'new song' put into his mouth by God after his deliverance from the pit (Psalm 40:2,3). Psalm 40 is itself the new song. The principle, however, is applicable to every occasion on which this command appears.

Again, although it may sound unusual, singing a new song can be understood sometimes as singing an *old song with a new perspective* – in much the same way as the 'new commandment' of Christ is really a new issuing of the 'old commandment' – from a 'new perspective' (1 John 2:7,8). Christ's new commandment – to 'love one another' – was hardly 'new' after all: it was binding under the Old Covenant and from the beginning of creation – but it came from Christ with new meaning and, doubtless, with new power. Similarly, each time a song attains a new fulfilment, it is sung again as a 'new song' without any alteration to its content.

For example, Psalm 98 is a post deliverance new song, as is Psalm 96. Both these psalms, however, attain to their fullest application in the proclamation of God's salvation and justice to the nations through the Gospel. Their language, even when it retains elements of the old order, is designed to accommodate that application – as we shall see later.

We see something similar in Isaiah. In Isaiah 12: 1-7, the prophet tells of God being praised by the nations in song. The content of such a song is revealed in verse 4 – which any regular singer of psalms will recognise from Psalm 105:1-2, a psalm which, to judge by its content, appears significantly to predate Isaiah himself. In other words, this functions as another case of a *canonical psalm becoming a 'new song' through the advent of Christ himself!*

> "The psalm which tells us to sing a new song *is itself* the new song!"

Psalms like this, and others, are indeed to be sung *to* and *by* the nations in evangelism and praise: 'Sing a new song to the Lord, all the earth sing to the Lord...show forth his salvation from day to day. Declare his glory to the nations and his wonders among the people' - Psalm 96:1-3.

Finally, in eschatological passages such as Isaiah 42:10, the call to sing a new song is practically reduced to a figure of speech rather than a direct command to sing as such; note that this song is to be sung by the sea creatures and the islands! Note also the well-known examples of trees and streams clapping their hands as they participate in the 'new songs' of Psalms 98 and 96! These songs took on further newness with advent of Christ and, as we shall see, require no supplementation.

All of the above demonstrates that the command to 'sing a new song to the Lord' does not, of itself, amount to a mandate to compose hymns for the worship of the church.

Before we leave this argument, however, we need to look at the presence of other scripture songs outside of the Book of Psalms. Again, we need to see what these songs are, and whether they are to be sung in the worship of the churches. This will allow us to deal with the vital issues of *canon* and *inspiration* and their bearing on what we should be singing in the worship of God.

Scripture Songs

The term 'Scripture songs' is, strictly, a reference to songs found within the Bible but not contained within the book of Psalms.

Such songs were considered for use in the church by the 1707 General Assembly of the Church of Scotland. However, the appetite for such songs in the 18th century Scottish church seemed to die away – indicating, perhaps, that it wasn't all that strong to begin with. However, with the rise of the Moderates (orthodox but non-evangelical Ministers), the clamour for change grew and resulted in the introduction of Paraphrases for singing later in the century. (By way of explanation, paraphrases are passages of scripture which are not songs but have been versified for the purpose of singing – in distinction from 'scripture songs' which were designed to be sung in the first place).

In the case of the Old Testament songs – such as those written by Moses, Hannah and Habakkuk – it is interesting that the advocates of singing new songs show remarkably little enthusiasm for using them in a manual of praise! Perhaps the main reason for this is that they add little to the songs of the Psalter: the substance of most of these songs is found elsewhere in the Book of Psalms.

As for the scripture songs of the New Testament, two things in particular need to be said.

First, if you read around these songs carefully, you will notice that none of these so-called scripture songs are referred to as songs in the Bible. We are not told that Mary, Elizabeth or Zacharias 'sang' anything. In fact it is rather absurd to think of Mary coming into her cousin's house and proceeding to sing the Magnificat! So, in spite of the common tendency to refer to them as songs, they are probably not to be thought of as songs at all.

Second, it is remarkable to note that, like the scripture songs of the Old Testament, *they add virtually nothing, by way of information, to the Psalms!* In a way, this is not surprising: although they appear in Luke's gospel, they are nonetheless old covenant songs and could really, in both form and content, be lifted straight from the psalter!

Now, this should give pause for thought to those who demand *new songs* to celebrate *new events*: the '*new event*' of Christ's birth produces supposed '*new songs*' from both Mary and Zacharias which are virtually indistinguishable, in form and content, from that of Hannah under the old covenant!

I wonder how many of those who profess a feeling of near gross deprivation at being unable to use the *Benedictus* or the *Magnificat* have really stopped to read them and to enquire as to how much further these 'songs' actually take them beyond the Psalms? Go on – read the *Magnificat* and then the Song of Hannah and you will see what I mean!

However, if it were to be granted that these compositions could pass for songs, then it is fair to say that the only ground on which they could be excluded from our sung worship today is that they appear to have been rejected from the final compilation of Psalms as found in the canonical Psalm book – a book which was closed, probably, by Ezra and never reopened by the Apostles. This raises the important and inter-related issues of canon and inspiration.

The importance of Canon and Inspiration

These issues of canon and inspiration should loom large in this whole discussion: after all, the songs of Moses, Deborah and others are held up by the advocates of new worship songs as examples of how we should compose such songs: using situations of triumph, grief or joy to produce materials of praise to God.

However, it needs more than competence in writing or attainments in godly living to justify the inclusion of our productions into the church's praise book! Rather, it requires inspiration by the Spirit as well as the express command of God to do so!

Consider, first of all, the issue of canon.

Canon

'Canon' is the term used to describe the books which are inspired scripture and are, as such, our rule (canon) of faith. They are the books that, collectively, make up the Bible: Genesis through to Revelation.

Crucially, the closing of the canonical Book of Psalms is tied in with the *ceasing of prophecy and inspired psalmody* until the advent of the Saviour. By the time of Christ, no inspired song *outside* of the canonical psalter appears to have been used in the temple service. Presumably, they would not have been used elsewhere, either – for example, in the Sabbath services of worship.

> "Significantly, the canon of psalms, compiled over a 1,500 year period, was not reopened by the Apostles to enable them to include the *Magnificat* or the *Benedictus*"

Significantly, the canon of psalms, compiled over a 1,500 year period, was not reopened by the Apostles to enable them to include the *Magnificat* or the *Benedictus*. This may be because the content of these 'songs' was already contained in the sung praise of the church or, as is more likely, because they were not actually 'songs' anyway – as I mentioned above, does anyone really believe that Mary called in to see Elizabeth and started singing? Or that Simeon sang with the child in his arms?

Clearly, then, while inspiration was essential for the inclusion of a song in the canonical psalm book, the mere presence of inspiration was not the sole criterion for including a song in the psalm book. *A song could be inspired but still left out of the canonical psalter!*

By way of example, Solomon wrote 1005 songs – however, only one or two of these appear to be included in the book of psalms. Of course, his 'Song of Songs' is included elsewhere, having its own distinctive place in the canon as the song par excellence. Solomon's father, David – presumably, as the 'sweet psalmist of Israel', a more prolific writer of songs than his son – writes most of the psalter, as is fitting for the typical Servant-King.

However, as well as writing other psalms referred to in the narrative of Samuel – which are not incorporated into the canonical psalm book – he must have written thousands of songs which don't appear in the psalm book either. Granted, we have no way of knowing how many of these were spiritual in nature, but the fact that they are not recorded in scripture is no reason to conclude that they were not.

Again, as indicated above, although inspiration is required for inclusion in the book of psalms, the mere fact that a song was inspired *did not mean that it therefore found its way into the psalm book*! For example, although Moses has at least three inspired songs included in scripture (Psalm 90, the song of Exodus 15 and the song of Deuteronomy 32), only the first of these was included in the book of Psalms. Similarly, many of David's songs are obviously included in the psalm book but his lament for Jonathan, as well as at least one other song recorded in the narrative of Samuel, is not. The same of course is true with the songs of Deborah, Hannah, Habakkuk and others.

As I have stated elsewhere, I am not sure why these songs were not included – especially when, in the case of Habakkuk, I am happy to acknowledge that the prayer was designed to be sung in the temple itself. It is possible that it was originally sung in the temple but that it ceased to be sung as the church was led to the formation of its canonical psalm book.

This shouldn't sound strange – after all, it is more than likely that a considerable amount of inspired apostolic speech and writings failed to find a permanent place in the New Testament canon also. Much was probably written and spoken by the Apostles which was inspired but didn't find its way into canonical scripture. This doesn't give us a license, however, to fill in the gaps ourselves!

This leaves us with what should seem fairly obvious anyway: the book of Psalms is compiled by the church, under the guidance and inspiration of God, to be *the psalm book of the church*. It is the church's book of praise. It is '*the book of psalms for singing*' designed to be sung by the church. That cannot be said of other passage of scripture which some may wish to convert into song material.

Inspiration

The connection between inspiration, canon and song raises a further issue as well. Perhaps we can highlight the issue by asking a question. How does the command to 'sing a new song' – a song which is inspired by the Spirit and composed by a prophet – become a command to us to compose and sing our own songs for worship in the new covenant church?

Some will argue that it simply stands to reason that we must compose our own songs after the events of crucifixion, resurrection, ascension and Pentecost. These events, it is claimed, simply demand new songs! Since the dispute in the Orthodox Presbyterian Church of America (OPC) on the issue of sung praise in the churches, much has been made of this particular argument: *new redemptive acts* in the Bible are always followed up by *new redemptive songs* – for example, the event of the exodus is followed by the song of Moses.

Those who argue in this way assert that the finished work of Christ, as *the* great redemptive act, should have its own outburst of song to follow it. The argument is apparently strengthened by an appeal to the outburst of song accompanying the incarnation. The argument runs as follows: if the birth of Christ is accompanied by the *Nunc Dimittis* and the *Magnificat,* surely Calvary must be followed by new songs more wonderful still?

The fact that they aren't followed by such songs – at least such songs don't appear in the Biblical record – would be explained by the advocates of new songs as a kind of call to ourselves, as spirit-filled Christians, to use our gifts in writing these songs and singing them. I don't think I would be doing any injustice to those who hold to this position to say that they would argue that the church is free, under the leading of the Holy Spirit, to compose as many songs in its worship as it wishes.

However, again, what appears convincing and straightforward is flawed! The real situation is a little more complex than that. The sequence behind the writing of new songs, under the old covenant, is not simply that of a *Redemptive Act* being followed by *Redemptive Song*. It is rather that of a *Redemptive Act* being followed by an *Inspired Song*!

Now some may claim that this is not fair: after all, they would say, the only reason we call these songs 'inspired songs' is because we find them in the Bible! If they weren't in the Bible, they wouldn't be inspired! So, they would say, if others can write songs then we can write them too - whether they appear in the Bible or not is a moot point!

However, this is to miss the point: the songs composed in celebration of redemptive events are not inspired *because they are included in the scripture*: rather, they are included in the scripture *because they are inspired*! There's a big difference! To be precise, the Holy Spirit hasn't just recorded these songs for us in the Bible: he has actually authored them for the particular occasion and for the use of the church.

It is important to understand this distinction: Some words are inspired simply because they appear in the Bible – and these include the lies of the Devil. Other words are in the Bible because they are inspired in the first place – such as the words of Christ. We don't know if other songs were written at the time of great redemptive acts in the Old and New Testaments but we do know that the ones which we have – such as Psalm 126 after the deliverance from captivity - were *commissioned and inspired by the Holy Spirit for the use of the church!*

To highlight this issue further, note carefully the following:

those who write the songs of the church are invariably prophets! For example, Moses, the author of the Exodus song, is a prophet; Miriam, a possible author, is a prophet also (Exodus 15:20, 21). Deborah, who composed her song, is another prophet (Judges 4:4 and 5); David is a prophet; crucially, *the officials overseeing the music and writing the songs of the temple service,* such as Heman, Asaph and Jeduthun, are prophets as well (see 1Chronicles 25:5 and 2 Chronicles 29:30, 35:15).

To extend this into the narrative of Luke (still, of course, under the old covenant), the utterances of Mary, Zacharias and Simeon are immediately inspired by the Holy Spirit. Moving into the new covenant, the charismatic psalms of 1 Corinthians 14 – assuming they are *new* compositions rather than choices of *existing* ones –are inspired by prophets also.

Are we getting the picture? What could be clearer? *The songs of the church are always inspired songs produced by prophets for the purpose of being sung in the churches!* The Reformed Churches have appeared to miss the point that creating new worship songs for the use of the church in worship is actually a *charismatic* activity – and have failed to spot the link between the rise of Pentecostal/ Charismatic phenomenon and the proliferation of worship songs.

It is significant to note in this particular discussion how Hezekiah behaves when he undertakes national reformation during his reign. He begins the work with a reformation of worship in the temple and when it comes to the matter of praise, the criterion he applies is simply *'what does the word of God authorise us to do?'* As we will see below, he re-instates the instruments of worship appointed by David. However, he also appoints the songs to be sung: 'Moreover, King Hezekiah and the leaders commanded the Levites to sing praise to the Lord *with the words of David and of Asaph the seer'* (2 Chronicles 29:30).

The importance of this can hardly be overstated: Hezekiah's kingdom would have plenty competent poets and musicians. However, because there were no songs composed by the inspiration of the Holy Spirit since the days of temple construction, *Hezekiah* felt compelled to use only those songs which had been inspired by the Holy Spirit some 300 years before! This is compelling evidence of the concern to use only the songs which the Holy Spirit has inspired in the worship of God.

We are nowhere told by God that this position has changed! If we need other songs under the New Covenant, apart from those we have, let a prophet inspired by the infallible Spirit of God write them! The claim that such a thing can be done belongs to Charismatic theology, not to Reformed theology.

> "If we need other songs under the New Covenant, apart from those we have, let a prophet inspired by the infallible Spirit of God write them!"

From all the above, we have seen that the command to 'sing a new song' does not allow us to create new songs for the worship of the church. This leads us to the second argument for the use of hymns which is that the Psalms are not sufficient.

II. 'THE PSALMS ARE NOT SUFFICIENT!'

Almost every plea for hymnody rests, at some point, on an alleged insufficiency attaching to the psalm book as a new covenant manual of praise. The reasoning is plain enough: if it is sufficient as a praise book, then why supplement it? In fairness, it should be understood that the deficiency attaching to the psalm book not to be understood in terms of what it is in itself, as a praise book, but strictly in how it functions as a new covenant manual of praise. The writer of the paper referred to at the outset makes this argument as well. As well as being frustrated with the lack of clarity in the psalms, just because they are written in advance, he says that he is:

> '...unhappy with the entire and exclusive stance on more strictly theological grounds...the exclusivist position ... claims one book of Old Testament Scripture as forever sufficient for our sung praise, rather than the whole canon. I do not believe in the sufficiency of the psalms alone for Christian praise...the psalms do not say many things we want to say in our new covenant song'

Do the Psalms say enough?

Before we deal with the issue of sufficiency itself, I wish to make the important point – not in any facetious manner – that what 'we want to say' in a new covenant song should never be the issue. I'm sure I know what the writer means by this, but it is still important to assert, always, that we are not the judges of what is fit to be sung in new covenant praise.

However, aside from this, many would feel that his case is plausible, and some would assert that his claim hardly requires proof. How could old covenant songs be adequate for a new covenant church anyway?

However, this argument fails because it doesn't do justice to the uniqueness of the Book of Psalms in the biblical revelation or, specifically, to the particular way in which the psalms are crafted by the Holy Spirit, who designed them with language specially fitted to accommodate the new covenant 'event' when it arrived. There are several ways to show this.

Christ in the Psalms

Not surprisingly, a lot of the discussion at this point will focus on the presence of Christ in the Psalms. Particularly, it will focus on whether he is there, the extent to which he is there and the clarity with which he can be seen.

It is perhaps as well to begin with a less obvious example: Christ singing in Matthew 26:30. It is more or less universally acknowledged that the psalm 'hymned' here is the Egyptian Hallel (Psalms 113-118) with the focus and climax being Psalm 118.

This psalm is not the easiest to interpret, but it is clearly Christ-centred (Acts 4:11). It bursts out into triumph from verse 15 onwards: the Day of the Lord (v24) has seen the arm of the Lord bringing salvation (v15) and rejoicing to God's people. It also opens the gates of righteousness into God's presence (v19). These gates are opened on the basis of the man whose claim to be the Christ was rejected by the 'builders' of God's house but who, nonetheless, through his sacrifice, becomes the very foundation-stone of God's temple (v22). The result is tremendous joy as the people welcome the Messiah into their midst (v26), while praying for the flourishing of his kingship (v25).

Now, this psalm, associated so closely with the both the coming of Christ as Saviour and the sacrament of the Passover, was applied by the multitudes to Christ as he rode into Jerusalem triumphantly on the donkey (Matthew 21:9). This was an all-too-rare instance of spiritual perception! However, the 'builders' of the church – the religious leaders of the day – reject his claim to Messiahship with the result that the prayer for the welfare of the Messiah, uttered by the crowd (Matthew 21:9) is apparently frustrated by the 'cutting off' of Messiah. However, as the Psalm describes, he would, in the Day of the Lord, be chosen to become the foundation stone after all (Acts 11:4). All this was somehow bound up with the Passover, for reasons which we can now understand.

Now, for our purposes, the interesting and indeed crucial point is this: as this psalm is taken up by Christ on his lips for the final time, he has just converted the old covenant Passover into the new covenant Lord's Supper.

However, he clearly feels no sense of discomfort, inadequacy or incongruity in taking up the same old covenant psalm on his lips! If the psalm was inadequate for the transition taking place, he, or the Spirit of God, would surely have provided new words. However, nothing of the kind is done.

Please note what is happening: the singing of the Psalm at the close of the first Lord's Supper has the function of *bringing* the Psalm as well as the meal into the new covenant!

"It seems strange that, at last, when the church can sing her covenant songs in the full light of the advent of her Servant-King, of whom they constantly speak, she wishes to supplement or abandon them!"

The simple fulfilment of Passover in Christ is enough to enable the Psalm to be sung intelligently – indeed, I would go so far as to say that the Psalm, from then on, could be sung as it had never been sung before. It became, effectively, a *'new song'*! Undoubtedly, the disciples were unable to sing it with the necessary illumination on that particular evening itself – it required the breathing of the Spirit, prior even to Pentecost, to illuminate the Psalms for them. However, the key point is that such illumination was *all that was required*.

With the passing of time, they would sing these wonderful verses with increasing appreciation and, certainly, without the need of supplement. *'I shall not die but live...set open the gate of righteousness...that stone has been made head of the corner...this is God's day and God's doing'*. Why would they need more? This Psalm, of course, continues to play its part at many communion tables just as it did at the first Lord's Supper 2000 years ago. Why supplement it? Worse still, why *replace* it?

This principle can be extended throughout the psalter. For example, it is difficult to see how Psalm 110 could be sung with proper comprehension under the old covenant:

'The Lord said to my Lord, 'sit at my right hand until I make your

enemies your footstool. The Lord will make the rod of your power extend from Zion – govern in the midst of your enemies! In your day of Power, from the very womb of its morning, a youthful, holy people, as fresh as dew, will come to you. By God's oath, you, the King, are a priest forever, according to Melchizedek's order.'

A moment's thought should reveal the difficulty of singing these words before the advent of Christ. The old covenant church must have been struggling, in a good sense, with these words – and perhaps their obscurity made them look forward, with a kind of holy envy, to those who would see them more clearly (I Peter 1:10-12). It seems strange that, at last, when the church can sing her covenant songs in the full light of the advent of her Servant-King, of whom they constantly speak, she wishes to supplement or abandon them!

We could go on in this way through the Psalm book to show that the facts regarding our Saviour's life and ministry are not dimly foreshadowed inside enigmas or riddles – as is often claimed to be the case - but *clearly stated in language from our Lord's own lips.* This language of Christ's was given to the prophets many years before for the benefit of the old covenant church and contemplates his work from the standpoint of the resurrection onwards: note that Psalm 110, referred to above, while written under the old covenant, speaks in plain language of events between the ascension and the consummation of all things. What more could one ask for?

Most Christians labour under the illusion that there are only a handful of Psalms which testify of Christ or which contain his words. The truth is quite different.

The resurrection, ascension, coronation and dominion of Christ are plain in Psalm 2, his exaltation to world-ruler in Psalm 8, his struggle in Gethsemane in Psalm 16, his distress in Psalm 20, his deliverance out of it and his glorification in Psalm 21, his distress and deliverance in his own feelings and words in Psalm 22, his leading of his people as their Shepherd/King in Psalm 23, his ascension to glory in Psalm 24, his incarnation, prophetic and priestly roles in Psalm 40, his betrayal in Psalm 41, his Kingship and Kingdom in Psalm 45, his ascension in Psalm 68, his universal Kingdom in Psalm 72, his intercession in Psalm 80, his preservation from evil in Psalm 91, his coming judgement and rule in Psalms 96 and 98, his Lordship in Psalm 102, his priestly Kingship in Psalm 110, and his resurrection and headship of the church in Psalms 118, 132 and 133 – and this list is not exhaustive.

Is Christ in them clearly enough?
However, even when the force of all this is felt, the claim persists that it is still not plain enough. But this is not the case! On the contrary, the clarity with which all this is brought before us cannot be over-emphasised: could the events of the crucifixion be any more poignantly, graphically or accurately portrayed than they are in the twenty-second Psalm – one which, with its piercings of hands and feet, must again have been deeply perplexing under the old covenant when crucifixions were unknown? All that is needed to bring it into the new covenant is the simple recognition of its fulfilment in Christ. Nothing more is needed! The language is graphic, plain and in the first person! I was present recently when an extended meditation on the crucifixion was brought to a conclusion by the singing of a hymn when the occasion of corporate worship so plainly cried out for the singing of Psalm 22!

This is important because frustration is sometimes felt with songs which apparently require 'too much explanation'. Apparently, people would rather songs which need less explanation than the Psalms do. However, this is foolish. All of the New Testament literature – including the gospel story – requires explanation and illumination. Have you tried reading the letter to the Ephesians to the proverbial 'man on the street'? *The church simply needs to grow up and begin to teach.*

What makes the Psalms unique is that they are not dark prophecy, shrouded in obscurity - as, for example, the tabernacle with its symbolism was so shrouded – but are, in fact, specially conceived by the Holy Spirit using extremely selective vocabulary and imagery to carry the church effortlessly into the new covenant and on through to the 'new song' of heaven itself.

In this respect, the Psalms are like a room full of intricate paintings of Christ. All we need to do to appreciate them is simply switch on the light. The light is provided by the Holy Spirit of the exalted Christ in heaven. We don't need any more pictures or, worse still, to throw them out and begin painting again ourselves. We just need to switch on the light – that's all!

Once this principle of illumination is grasped, the precise function of the Psalms as the church's songbook and its adequacy in that capacity under the new covenant, becomes plainer. Indeed, once this principle is properly grasped, the whole case against the sufficiency of the psalm book collapses!

Do the Psalms say too much?

However, another issue needs dealing with and, surprisingly, is doesn't really concern the Psalms saying too little but the Psalms saying too much!

It is increasingly difficult to escape the conclusion that the desire to supplement or replace the psalms often proceeds from a discomfort with their theology. Sad to say, this discomfort appears in the paper advocating hymnody referred to above.

It comes out when the writer goes on to highlight what he sees as the unsuitability of some old covenant songs for new covenant use. In this connection, he makes the following remarkable statement:

> '*I am far from suggesting that all the songs should be sung in our services, and for example I struggle to see how a metrical version of Judges 5:24-30 would make our praise more attractive and accessible. I have no wish to sing blessings on Jael, with her bowl of curdled milk and her skill with hammer and tent peg, or to recount the cries of Sisera's mother and her speculations about the spoils and 'a girl or two for each man'.*

Surely, I am not the only one who has a serious difficulty with this kind of thinking?

First, is it wise or right to state, as the writer does, that 'I have no wish to sing blessings on Jael' - when God himself has told us to bless her? Deborah, the prophetess, calls Jael 'blessed among women' and yet the writer can say that he has no wish to bless her!

Second, is it really the case that we should contemplate leaving an inspired song out of our worship on the ground that it may not be 'attractive' or 'accessible' enough? Is it not strange that after spending his strength trying to build a case for singing things that aren't really songs in the first place, the writer then comes across a song in the Bible, inspired by a prophetess, and he 'has no wish to sing' it?

Significantly, it is vital to note that the kinds of things which the writer cites as being unattractive and inaccessible (Jael's tent peg and hammer) are things which *must render huge portions of the psalms equally unattractive and inaccessible to him as well!* Was this not precisely why Isaac Watts deliberately set out to 'Christianise' the psalms by rewriting them and removing what was supposedly inconsistent with the spirit of the new covenant?

But, in any case, who are we to judge the *attractiveness* of what God has inspired? Surely, when you begin to feel uncomfortable with the songs God has written, what you really need to do is not advocating new songs but examine your theology and the state of your heart!

Sadly, there is a sense in which these kinds of statements let the proverbial cat out of the bag: In spite of all the praise being heaped upon the psalms by the advocates of hymnody, and the requisite re-affirmations of their supreme value and peerless place in our worship – which invariably take the form of 'I love the Psalms *but*' – I cannot help feeling that there is considerable discomfort with them – and with some of their theological emphases in particular.

In an age of declension, the obsession is now with what is 'attractive' and 'accessible'. It is hard to conceive of a more unspiritual approach. Instead of choking on the difficult bits and refusing to bless people with hammers and tent pegs, surely we should urgently rediscover the Psalms as the *praise book revealing God's Servant-King* and begin to teach it as well as sing it *with its own emphases*: the Servant-King's worldwide dominion, his righteousness, his judgement, his salvation, his peace, his goodness and his worship!

"The singing of the Psalms in a spiritual and intelligent manner, in the light of their fulfilment in and by Christ, is probably the single greatest aid to edification that I know"

The sad fact is that the Psalms ceased to be properly understood and properly sung in Scottish Reformed Churches a long time ago. For far too long, they have been apologetically held as a praise book, unintelligently used and poorly sung. Sadly, in the case of some churches, their full-orbed Reformed theology finds little acceptance because a weaker and more general evangelical sentiment now reigns.

Alleged Deficiencies

The writer of the paper I have been referring to closes by issuing five please for hymnody on the grounds of *edification, ecumenism, evangelism, emotion and exultation*. In all of these areas, he argues that the sung praise of the church will be defective if it relies on the psalms alone. I could hardly disagree more.

As to *edification*, it is difficult to make up for the lack of a good Psalm book – well memorised and often sung. The singing of the Psalms in a spiritual and intelligent manner, in the light of their fulfilment in and by Christ, is probably the single greatest aid to edification that I know. Nothing forms the piety of a people as well as this (see Athanasius and his letter to Marcellinus referred to above). Here, it needs to be emphasised that the current trend to produce too many versions of the Psalter is as damaging to the memorisation of song as the production of too many versions of scripture is to scripture memorisation generally.

As to *ecumenism*, it is a notorious fact that hymnody, in the past at least, has been denominational, partisan and exclusive. The hymns and songs which do not fall so easily into these categories now are, not surprisingly, the least radical, the most celebratory and the least offensive of them. *Contemporary hymnody is alarmingly anaemic.* It is almost, if not altogether, devoid of any teaching respecting judgment or hell. More than any other genre or collection of songs, the Psalms belong to the *church catholic* and for whatever reason – and I could suggest a few – they are more valued in the oldest communions on the earth than in those which are 'Reformed'.

As regards *evangelism*, it is worth stating that the church's primary role, in its Lord's Day worship, is not an evangelistic one – at least as 'evangelism' is commonly understood. It is rather to offer her covenantal tribute of worship to her Lord. That is not to say that evangelism is no part of her role, nor is it to say that the offering of her tribute is not, itself, evangelistic.

Unsurprisingly, there is probably an underlying assumption here about what God uses in evangelising and what evangelism really is: contemporary theological culture finds 'kiss the Son in case you perish in his anger' (Psalm 2) to be an unacceptable or 'inaccessible' form of evangelism whereas 'come to Jesus' always hits the mark. This says a lot about current views of Christ (who is now almost invariably, and not without reason, replaced by '*Jesus*' – have you ever stopped to think why '*Christ*' is now always '*Jesus*'?) and indicates a definite change in how the gospel is viewed. The Psalms simply *are* evangelistic. They do not need to contain manufactured appeals in our contemporary acceptable forms for them to qualify as such!

As to *emotion*, while the writer acknowledges that the whole range is covered in the Psalms, he nonetheless believes that the singing of the Psalms alone in worship leaves us emotionally deprived or stunted. I just cannot agree. I find a depth of emotion, in connection with the worship of the Saviour as he is in the Psalms, which I fail to find absolutely anywhere else. I increasingly find as I *go on* and, hopefully, *grow on* in the Christian pilgrimage, that only the Psalms will do. In my *real* lows and in my *real* highs, it is invariably to them I turn, instinctively so, and it is their language I find myself expressing. And, for whatever reason, the pleasure I have in singing different kinds of songs at different times would completely evaporate if I were to import them, particularly at the expense of the psalms, into the worship of God.

As for *exultation*, the writer says that *'...it is central to our theology of worship that we share now in the worship of heaven. We are part of that fellowship and worship (Hebrews 12:22-24), and so we lift up heart and voice to join with the redeemed and with the angelic host around the throne.'* Indeed – but did that only commence under the new covenant? Even he must have noticed that the worship of heaven in Revelation is described with the symbolism of the old covenant! Coming to Mount Zion, in Hebrews 12, surely means something more than this!

Finally, although it should hardly need saying, doing God's will on earth as it is done in heaven does not necessarily mean that *his will for the two places is exactly the same*: We are all in the dark as to what, precisely, he wills of the members of his church in heaven as to their work, their appearance, their speech and, of course, their song – apart from the glimpses in Revelation. We don't even know which language he wills them to sing it in! Our concern, of course, should be with doing his will for us *on the earth* – and to do *that* as it is done in heaven: that is, immediately, without reservation and well. If this means singing the songs of the church militant until we get to sing the songs of the church at home and triumphant, we should be delighted to do so.

CONCLUSION

The very least which can be said, then, is that the case for singing hymns is far from proven. And, for a person truly Reformed in approach and, therefore, jealous not to intrude into worship anything that lacks express authority from God, that should be enough. However, this is only the least that should be said and, in reality, it is nowhere near enough.

It is more needful and correct to say that the case for singing only the Biblical Psalms is *well proven*! It follows that the church badly needs to repent in this area and rediscover this truth which she once held and professed but has now largely forsaken – to her great cost.

Rev. Kenneth Stewart is the minister of the Glasgow congregation of the Reformed Presbyterian Church of Scotland.

II.

The Singing of Psalms in the Worship of God

William Maclean

'*Let the word of Christ dwell in you richly in all wisdom; teaching and admonishing one another in psalms and hymns and spiritual songs, singing with grace in your hearts unto the Lord*' (Colossians 3:16).

When there are differences of view among Christians on any subject, it is always helpful to inquire how far they agree, and thus ascertain the exact point at which opinions begin to diverge. In regard to the songs to be employed in the praise of God, there are several points of general agreement.

Points of Agreement

+ It is agreed that the Psalms were given by Divine inspiration and are the very Word of God. 'David the son of Jesse said, and the man *who was* raised up on high, the anointed of the God of Jacob, and the sweet psalmist of Israel, said, The Spirit of the Lord spake by me, and His word *was* in my tongue' (2 Samuel 23:1-2).

'Men *and* brethren, this scripture must needs have been fulfilled, which the Holy Ghost by the mouth of David spake before concerning Judas, which was guide to them that took Jesus' (Acts 1:16. See also Acts 4:25; Heb 3:7 *et al*). Men should be careful how they speak against the Book of Psalms. The Holy Ghost is its author. This is the first point of agreement.

It is agreed that these inspired Psalms were appointed by God to be used in His worship. 'Sing unto Him, sing psalms unto Him' (1 Chronicles 16:9). 'Moreover, Hezekiah, the king and the princes commanded the Levites to sing praise unto the Lord with the words of David, and of Asaph the seer' (2 Chronicles 29:30). 'Let us come before His presence with thanksgiving and make a joyful noise unto Him with psalms' (Psalm 95:2). Bible expositors and Church historians alike agree that the inspired Psalms were exclusively used in the worship of the Old Testament. God appointed them to be so used, and no one but God could change the appointment. This is the second point of agreement.

It is agreed that so far as the record goes our Lord Jesus Christ used the Psalms exclusively in Worship. Only on one occasion is our Lord referred to as singing. This was in connection with the observance of the Passover. It is said, 'And when they had sung a hymn they went out into the Mount of Olives' (Matthew 26:30; Mark 14:26). Biblical scholars are not misled by the use of the word 'hymn' in our translation of this verse. The original simply states the fact that they sang praises to God. In the margin it reads, 'When they had sung a psalm'. It is a well-known fact that the Jews were accustomed to sing at the Passover the great Hallel, which consisted of Psalms 113 to 118 inclusive. Certainly our Lord and His apostles did not depart from this usage. Strange indeed it would have been if the Lord Jesus, Who always exalted and honoured the Holy Spirit, had put aside the sacred songs which He indited for this very purpose. But he did not. Those who would follow closely in the footsteps of Jesus should sing Psalms. This is the third point of the agreement.

✦ It is agreed that we have express authority for the use of the Old Testament Psalms in the New Testament Church. 'Let the word of Christ dwell in you richly in all wisdom, teaching and admonishing one another in psalms and hymns and spiritual songs, singing with grace in your hearts unto the Lord' (Colossians 3:16). Whatever differences of view there may be as to the 'hymns and spiritual songs', all agree that the Psalms here spoken of are the inspired Psalms of Scripture. The passage therefore contains an express warrant for the continued use of the Psalter in the New Testament Church. This is not denied by any one. This is the fourth point of agreement.

It is not affirmed that there are no opinions contrary to one or another of these four points, held by individuals, but that there is a general agreement among all classes of evangelical Christians on these points.

I. NO WARRANT FOR HYMNS

We have now reached the exact point of divergence. While all agree that the 'psalms' referred to in Colossians 3:16 are the Bible Psalms, there are many who maintain that the 'hymns and spiritual songs' are mere human compositions: and that the New Testament Church is hereby authorised and instructed to add to her book of praises the writings of uninspired men. This is the crucial text on this subject. If this text contains a clear warrant for the use of uninspired hymns, other passages may lend it support; but if that warrant is not found here it is not found anywhere. The advocates of hymn singing will admit the truth of this statement. It is now undertaken to show that not only does this passage not authorise the use of uninspired songs in worship, but that it enjoins the exclusive use of the Psalms of the Bible.

> "'Spiritual songs' are songs produced in a supernatural manner, those given immediately by the Spirit of God"

No warrant can be found for the use of uninspired songs, in the words 'hymns and spiritual songs'. At first view these words seem to be conclusive in favour of the advocates of hymn-singing. In the Greek text it is 'psalmois, humnois, odais pneumatikais' – i.e., 'psalms, hymns, songs, spiritual'. Now these three Greek names are all found in the titles to the Psalms in the Greek translation of the Old Testament which was in use among the people to whom Paul wrote this epistle. They occur many times in the titles to the various Psalms. The word 'psalmois' about sixty-three times; the word 'humnois' six times, and another word, 'alleluia' which has precisely the same import, about twenty times; and the word 'odais' (mostly in the singular form) thirty-four times. With the fact before us that these three words are all actually found many times in the titles to the inspired Psalms – and when we all agree that the word 'psalmois' does refer to inspired songs – is it not most unreasonable to insist that 'humnois and odais' mean uninspired songs? As if to remove all possible doubt the word 'spiritual' is used to qualify the words. Thayer, in his Lexicon of the New Testament, referring to this passage and the similar one – Ephesians 5:19 – defines the word 'spiritual' as 'divinely inspired and so redolent of the Holy Spirit'.

Dr. Albert Barnes in his commentary on 1 Corinthians 10:3, 'And did all eat the same spiritual meat; and did all drink the same spiritual drink', says: 'The word "spiritual" is evidently used to denote that which is given by the Spirit, by God; that which was the result of His miraculous gift; that which was not produced in the ordinary way'. Again, 'The word "spiritual" must be used in the sense of supernatural, or that which is immediately given by God'. Hence 'spiritual songs' are songs produced in a supernatural manner, those given immediately by the Spirit of God. It is just as if it read, 'Teaching and admonishing one another, in psalms and hymns and songs, given by the Holy Spirit'. What songs are these? The sweet psalmist of Israel answers: 'The Spirit of the Lord spake by me, and his word was in my tongue'. These very names, therefore, which have been relied upon as furnishing a warrant for the use of uninspired songs, we find to be well-known titles for the Psalms of the Bible, and that as qualified by the word 'spiritual' they cannot be used to designate uninspired songs but furnish a warrant for the exclusive use of the songs of the Spirit.

II. THE PSALMS THE WORD OF CHRIST

The Psalms are in an eminent sense 'the word of Christ'. 'Let the word of Christ dwell in you richly in all wisdom'. This is the condition of being able to teach and admonish.

How are the Psalms "the word of Christ"?

1. Christ by His Spirit is the **author** of them. This has been fully shown above.

2. Christ is the **speaker** in many of them. For instance "I will declare the decree; the Lord said unto Me, Thou art my Son; this day have I begotten Thee" (Psalm 2:7). 'Then said I, Lo, I come: in the volume of the book it is written of Me' (Psalm 40:6). 'My God, my God, why hast Thou forsaken Me?' (Psalm 22:1). Such Psalms as these are 'the word of Christ' in the same sense that the Sermon on the Mount is His word. He and no one else is the speaker in them.

3. Christ alone is the **subject** of many of them. The most ignorant and senseless objection ever made to the Psalms is the

charge that they are 'Christless'. The truth is that no book in the Bible reveals Christ with such fullness as is done in the book of Psalms, not excepting the Gospel according to John or the Epistle to the Hebrews.

What may we learn of Christ in this wonderful book?
    1. His **Divinity**. Psalm 14:6, 'Thy Throne, O God, is for ever and ever', (compared with Hebrews 1:8). Psalm 110:1: 'The Lord said unto my Lord, sit Thou at my right hand until I make thine enemies thy footstool', (compared with Matthew 22:42-45).
    2. His Eternal **Sonship**. Psalm 2:7, 'I will declare the decree; the Lord said unto Me, Thou art my Son; this day have I begotten Thee', (compared with Hebrews 1:5).
    3. His **Incarnation**. Psalm 8:5, 'For thou hast made Him a little lower that the angels, and hast crowned Him with glory and honour', (compared with Hebrews 2:9). Psalm 11:7, 'Then said I, Lo, I come; in the volume of the book it is written of Me'. (compared with Hebrews 10:5-7).
    4. His **Mediatorial Offices**.
(a) His **Prophetical** office. Psalm 11:9-10, 'I have preached righteousness in the great congregation' etc.; Psalm 22:22, 'I will declare they name unto my brethren', (compared with Hebrews 2:12).
(b) His **Priestly** office. Psalm 110:4, 'The Lord hath sworn, and will not repent; Thou art a priest for ever after the order of Melchizedec', (compared with Hebrews 7:17).
(c) His **Kingly** office. Psalm 14:6, 'Thy throne, O God is for ever and ever; the sceptre of thy kingdom is a right sceptre', (compared with Hebrews 1:8). Psalm 110:1, 'The Lord said unto my Lord, Sit Thou at my right hand until I make thine enemies thy footstool', (compared with Matthew 22:42-45; Hebrews 1:13). See also Psalm 22:28, and Psalm 72 throughout.
    5. His **Betrayal**. Psalm 41:9, 'Yea, mine own familiar friend, in whom I trusted which did eat my bread, hath lifted up his heel against Me', (compared with John 23:18).

6. His **Agony in the Garden**. Psalm 22:2, 'O my God, I cry in the daytime, but Thou hearest not; and in the night season, and am not silent', (compared with Hebrews 5:7).

7. His **Trial**. Psalm 35:11, 'False witnesses did rise up; they laid to my charge things that I knew not', (compared with Matthew 26:59-60).

8. His **Rejection**. Psalm 22:6, 'But I am a worm, and no man; a reproach of men, and despised of the people', (compared with Matthew 27:21-23; Luke 23:18-23). Psalm 118:22, 'The stone which the builders refused is become the headstone of the corner', (compared with Matthew 21:42; Acts 4:11-12).

9. His **Crucifixion**. Psalm 22 throughout, also Psalm 69, (compared with the Gospels). The scenes attending the crucifixion are described to the minutest particulars. The mockery, the shaking the head, the parting the garments, the casting lots on the vesture, the thirst, the vinegar and the gall, the pierced hands and feet, the cry of the forsaken, the committing of His Spirit to God, and the 'It is finished', as many read the last verse of Psalm 22.

10. His **Burial and Resurrection**. Psalm 16:9-11, 'For Thou wilt not leave my soul in hell; neither wilt Thou suffer thine Holy One to see corruption. Thou wilt show Me the path of life', etc. (compared with Acts 2:25-31).

11. His **Ascension**. Psalm 47:5, 'God is gone up with a shout, the Lord with the sound of the trumpet', (compared with Acts 1:11, and 1 Thessalonians 4:16). Psalm 68:18, 'Thou hast ascended on high, Thou hast led captivity captive; Thou hast received gifts for men; yea, for the rebellious also, that the Lord God might dwell among them', (compared with Ephesians 4: 8-10). Psalm 24:7-10, 'Lift up your heads, O ye gates; and be ye lift up, ye everlasting doors; and the King of glory shall come in', etc., (compared with Revelation 5:6-14).

12. His **Second Coming**. Psalm 50:3-4, 'Our God shall come, and shall not keep silence. He shall call to the heavens from above, and to the earth, that he may judge his people'. Psalm 98:6-9, 'With trumpets and sound of cornet make a joyful noise before

the Lord, the King. Before the Lord; for He cometh to judge the earth; with righteousness shall he judge the world, and the people with equity', (compared with Matthew 24:31; 1 Corinthians 15:52). Well said Jesus, It is written 'in the Psalms, concerning Me'. 'The sufferings of Christ, and the glory that should follow', are here unfolded, and these 'psalms and hymns and spiritual songs' are replete with Christ. If anyone will examine and compare these passages, he will readily believe that when Paul wrote, 'let the word of Christ, dwell in you richly in all wisdom' it was as if he had said, 'Memorise the Psalms'.

III. THE PSALMS A VEHICLE OF INSTRUCTION

Uninspired songs could not be placed on a level with the songs of inspiration as the rule for 'teaching and admonishing'. All agree that the 'psalms' of the text are the inspired psalms, the very word of God. 'Teaching' refers to Doctrine – what we are to believe. 'Admonishing' refers to Practice – how we are to live. It is not conceivable that Paul would place the writings of uninspired men on a level with the Psalms of the Bible as a standard of doctrine and practice. 'The holy Scriptures of the Old and New Testament are the word of God, the only rule of faith and obedience' – Westminster Larger Catechism.

Uninspired hymns abound in errors. Dr. H. Cooke, of Belfast, said he never had found a compilation of hymns that he 'could pronounce free from serious doctrinal errors'. In 1836, the old school Presbyterian General Assembly (U.S.) appointed a Committee to revise their hymn-book. In their report they say: 'On a critical examination we found many hymns deficient in literary merit, some incorrect in doctrine, and many altogether unsuitable for the sanctuary'. What an indictment to bring against the book which their own Church had substituted for God's book of praises! Does anyone suppose that Paul referred to such 'hymns and spiritual songs' as these, and placed them on a level with the Psalms of the Bible for 'teaching and admonishing?'

Can the Christian reader believe that Paul pointed to

these as standards of doctrine and practice of equal authority with the Psalms for teaching and admonishing? No, no. Paul never played fast and loose with the doctrines of the gospel. He says: 'Though we, or an angel from heaven, preach any other gospel unto you than that which we have preached unto you, let him be accursed' (Galatians 1:8). If there was no other argument to show that the 'hymns and spiritual songs' in which Christians are to teach and admonish one another are not mere human compositions, this would be conclusive. Paul was not advising the propagation of error.

> "The Psalms are objective. They are God-centred. The soul looks outward and upward. They lead the soul reverently to adore God 'in the beauty of holiness', as the object of praise, and devoutly to bow before Him on His throne, as the hearer of prayer"

IV. THE PSALMS A VEHICLE OF GRACE

The inspired Psalms alone are adapted to be vehicles of grace to the heart, and of praise to the Lord. 'Singing with grace in your hearts unto the Lord'. Here we have the end to be reached. It is twofold: (1) Awakening of gracious affections in the heart, and (2) the uplifting of the soul to God. Two characteristics of the inspired Psalms mark their adaptation to this twofold purpose, viz., (a) their objective nature, and then (b) their devotional spirit. Hymns are subjective. Men sing about themselves, their states and experiences, their high resolves. Hymns are introspective. They are self-centred.

The Psalms are objective. They are God-centred. The soul looks outward and upward. They lead the soul reverently to adore

God 'in the beauty of holiness', as the object of praise, and devoutly to bow before Him on His throne, as the hearer of prayer. This is true devotion. 'Worship God'.

The devotional character of the book is manifest to all. This is in a pre-eminent sense the devotional book of the Bible. It is sometimes asserted that the Psalms are not adapted to be the vehicles of grace to the heart, and, therefore, they cannot be successfully employed in religious revivals! Such a view is utterly mistaken.

Think for a moment of the contents of the book. Its views of God; its views of man; its views of law; its views of sin; its views of Christ; its views of repentance; its views of pardon; its views of Covenant-relationship; its views of the new life; its views of judgement; its views of heaven; its views of hell. What is there that is needed for revival that it does not contain? And what book is more likely to be honoured by the Holy Spirit than His own book? As Dr. J. Bain has said, the Psalms 'will be found suitable for any revival that comes down; those revivals that are "gotten up" may need something less divine'.

The fact is that the greatest revivals of religion the world has ever seen have been connected with the exclusive use of the Psalms. They were used exclusively in the great revivals in the days of Hezekiah, Josiah, Ezra, Nehemiah. The same was true in the revival at Pentecost when 3000 were converted in one day. The period of the Reformation was a grand revival period, and it was a glorious revival of Psalm-singing. The Calvinistic Reformers used the Psalms exclusively. All France was thrilled with their music in the days of the Huguenots. They alone were used in the Scottish Church on that wonderful day at the Kirk o' Shotts when under Livingston 500 were converted by one sermon. In the times of Robert McCheyne, when the Disciples of Christ continued their meetings until near midnight, they made the seasons of the night glad singing the Songs of Zion.

President Edwards bears testimony as to their use in the great Northampton revival in New England in his days. 'One of the most observable features of the work was the singular delight which all the awakened appeared to take in singing Psalms. In houses, in the fields, in the woods, alone and together, they spake forth the praise of their King; and even little children and aged persons who had never before learned to sing, came to sing praises with solemnity and sweetness'. It thus appears that the Psalms of the Bible are eminently adapted to be the vehicles of grace to the heart and of praise to the Lord. 'Singing with grace in your hearts to the Lord'.

We conclude, therefore, that this passage, which has always been relied upon by the advocates of hymn-singing as containing a warrant for their practices, has no such meaning. The titles, "Psalms and hymns and spiritual songs", belong to the inspired Psalms, and as qualified by the word "spiritual" are not true of any other. The Psalms are the word of Christ; uninspired songs are not His word; the Psalms are true standard for "teaching and admonishing"; uninspired songs are not; the Psalms are adapted to be the vehicles of grace to the heart and of praise to the Lord' uninspired songs are not.

The passage furnishes no warrant for the use of uninspired songs in worship, but is an explicit apostolic injunction that in the praise service of the New Testament Church the divinely authorised Psalmody should be continued.

CONCLUSION

We cannot close without an earnest appeal to the Christian heart in behalf of two things.

1. The restoration of God's own Psalter to a place in the hymnals of all the Churches. The present movement in this direction should have the hearty co-operation of every Christian. Its rejection has been in disregard of the divine appointment, and of example of our blessed Lord, and of the apostolic authority contained in this passage. It should be restored to its place by the united voice of all Christendom and the joyous acclaim of all Christians. It would be the bringing back of the ark of God.

2. When the Psalter is restored to its place in the hymnals of the Churches it should be used EXCLUSIVELY in the worship of God. A place may be found for the use of uninspired songs, but not in worship. God must be served with His own. 'But cursed be the deceiver, which hath his flock a male, and voweth and sacrificeth unto the Lord a corrupt thing: for I am a great King saith the Lord of hosts, and my name is dreadful among the heathen' (Malachi 1:14).

Rev. William Maclean was the minister of the congregations of the Free Presbyterian Church of Scotland in Gisborne (New Zealand), Grafton (Australia), and Ness, Isle of Lewis. He died in 1985.

USEFUL QUOTES

Rev. W. D. Ralston in 'Talks on Psalmody' relates the following story. 'As I trudged homewards, I stopped at an uncle's, and spent the night there. In the evening I brought out my hymn-book and had some singing with my cousins. After I laid it down, my uncle took it up, put on his glasses and spent some time in looking through it. He was a firm believer in the exclusive use of Psalms, and my book was the hymn-book of another denomination. It gave the hymns, and the music, with the names of the composers of each as far as known. Uncle read a hymn, and, naming the author said, "I know nothing of him". He read another and said, "I have read about the author of this one. He was a Roman Catholic Priest. He read another and said: "I have often read of this author. He was a good man and an earnest Christian minister". He then said: "Now, John, if I were going to use one of these hymns in the worship of God tonight, which do you think I had best choose, the one about whose author I knew nothing, the one by the Roman Catholic Priest, or the one by the earnest Christian minister"? I replied, "The one by the minister." "True", said he, "we should select the one written by the best man; and I see by looking through your book that it contains many hymns written by good men; but if I should find in it one composed by God Himself, would it not be better to sing than the one composed by any good man?" I replied, "It surely would". After a little he said, "I have now carefully looked through your book, and I do not find one hymn in it marked – Composed by God; but I have here a little hymn-book, and God by His Holy Spirit has composed every hymn in it; Peter says – Holy men of God spake as they were moved by the Holy Ghost". As he spoke, he handed me one of our Psalm-books, and the manner in which he presented his argument made an impression upon my mind that I never forgot'.

How conclusive the argument is. We ought to serve God with the best. God's own book is the best. When Ingersol said that he 'could write a better book than the Bible', Christians were shocked, and denounced him as an 'infidel blasphemer'. How, then, can we say that we can write a better book of praises than God's Psalter? If it be true that hymn-books are better than the Psalm-book it marks the highest achievement of the race for then man has transcended God in his own field! If it be not true, then the displacing of the God-made Psalter by the man-made hymn-books in God's worship is an act of most daring presumption.

At a meeting of ministers of various denominations in an eastern city, a paper had been read on church-hymnology. General discussion followed the reading. An advocate of the exclusive use of the inspired Psalms employed the following illustration with great effect! 'If I had an important message to send to one living in the upper districts of the city, I might summon a messenger boy and say to him "Can you carry this message for me to such a person, living in such a part of the city"? And the boy would answer doubtfully: "I think I can. It is true, I have never been in that part of the city. I was born near here. I have heard of the person to whom you wish to send the message, but I am not acquainted with him: but I think I can find him. I am willing to try". My message is a very important one, and while satisfied of the good intentions of this boy, I am not quite assured of his ability to fulfil the trust. So I call up another boy, and ask him the same question. At once his face glows with intelligence as he answers: "O yes, I can carry your message directly to his home. I know all about that part of the city. I was born there. I came from there here. In fact, your friend sent me down here to find you and bear up any message you might desire to send him. It would not be difficult to decide which of these messengers I should employ. This is an allegory. If I had a message of praise to send to God, and I employed a hymn to carry it, I would feel uncertain about it; it might reach Him, and it might not. But if I employed a Psalm to carry it I know that it would ascend to heaven. The Psalm was born there. It came from God to me; and indeed God sent it to me to bear any message of praise I might wish to send to Him'.

- Rev. Robert J. George, D.D.

'I want a name for that man who should pretend that he could make better hymns than the Holy Ghost. His collection is large enough; it wants no addition. It is as perfect as its Author, and not capable of any improvement. Why, in such a case, would any man in the world take it into his head to sit down and write hymns for the use of the Church? It is just the same as if he were to write a new Bible, not only better than the old, but so much better that the old may be thrown aside. What a blasphemous attempt! And yet our hymn-mongers, inadvertently I hope, have come very near to this blasphemy; for they shut out the Psalms, to introduce their own verses into the Church, sing them with great delight, and, as they fancy with great profit; although the practice be in direct opposition to the command of God, and, therefore, cannot possibly be accompanied with the divine blessing.'

-William Romaine

Q2: *What rule hath God given to direct us how we may glorify and enjoy Him?*
A: The Word of God, which is contained in the Scriptures of the Old and New Testaments, is the only rule to direct us how we may glorify and enjoy Him. (Proof text: 2 Timothy 3:16).

-Westminster Shorter Catechism

Songs of the Spirit

III.

Christ in All the Psalms

Donald Balfour

Every Christian believer knows the blessing of Christ being revealed to his soul in certain verses of the book of Psalms. We have examples in verse 1 of Psalm 22: 'My God, my God, why hast thou forsaken me?' and in verses 7 and 8 of Psalm 40: 'Then said I, Lo, I come: in the volume of the book *it is* written of me, I delight to do thy will, O my God'; or verse 1 of Psalm 110: 'The Lord said unto my Lord, sit thou at my right hand'.

But it is a far greater matter of awe to discern Christ in every one of the 150 Psalms! Are we not brought to think of this in the Upper Room after the resurrection of Christ when he declares to His disciples, 'that all things must be fulfilled which were written in the law of Moses, and *in* the prophets, and *in* the psalms, concerning me' (Luke 24: 44)? The next statement of Holy Scripture immediately following this is vital: 'Then opened he their understanding, that they might understand the scriptures' (Luke 24:45). Let us pray individually for this understanding. Then we will be brought close to Christ from Psalm 1 to Psalm 150.

We can consider together some less well-known examples of the life of Christ Jesus in the Psalms.

The Sinless Christ

In His early life, Jesus was altogether without sin (Hebrews 2:15). His was a life of holy perfection (Hebrews 9:26). This helps to open up a Psalm like Psalm 139 which enables us to see the words of the Psalm as the words of Christ to his Father. It is Christ (more than David) who utters the words, 'Search me, O God, and know my heart: try me, and know my thoughts: and see if *there be any* wicked way in me, and lead me in the way everlasting' (Psalm 139: 23-24). Wonderful! There are other Psalms in which the purity of the upright man is brought before us in such a way that we can only conclude that it must be Christ. For example, in Psalm 1:3, we cannot avoid the conclusion that we are pointed to Christ: there is no other person than Christ of whom it can properly be said, 'his leaf also shall not wither, and whatsoever he doeth shall prosper'.

The Sin-bearing Christ

But we stop with greater wonder when we ponder the implications of these great words in the New Testament, when we read that God 'hath made him *to be* sin for us, who knew no sin; that we might be made the righteousness of God in him' (2 Corinthians 5:21). It is when we receive this by faith that we begin to expand in our love of Jesus our Saviour, as he is revealed more and more in the Psalms. Even those clearly Messianic Psalms in which the writer suddenly speaks of himself as sinful before God – even these words are best understood as still being the words of Christ. In Psalm 69, we have Christ speaking plainly – but, suddenly, he says 'Lord, thou my folly know'st, my sins not cover'd are from thee' (Psalm 69:5). Is this still Christ speaking? Yes it is – now as our sin-bearer 'made to be sin for us'. He is not a sinner personally – but he is loaded with our sins for which he is personally guilty.

The Obedient Christ

These examples shed light on other Psalms and other situations in which our Saviour found himself. Let's take his obedience. If we meditate on the truth that Jesus 'though he were a Son, yet learned he obedience' (Hebrews 5:8) we can then recognise the song of Christ in Psalm 119 as He cries out to God to be taught and kept: 'Thy word have I hid in mine heart, that I might not sin against thee' (Psalm 119:11) and 'Teach me, O Lord, the way of thy statutes' (Psalm 119:33). There can be no-one who can say with such truthfulness as Christ can 'O how love I thy law! It *is* my meditation all the day' (Psalm 119:97).

The Worshipping Christ

Throughout his earthly ministry the Son of God led a life of worship and prayer. The Bible records that it was His faithful delight to join in the worship of the synagogue on the Sabbath (Matthew 12:9, 13:54; Mark 1:21; Luke 4:16 and John 6:59). While engaged in worship, Jesus would have sung the Psalms – every one of them – and in doing so, he would take the 'I' and 'me' of the psalmist to himself. For example, 'I cried unto the Lord with my voice' (Psalm 3:4) and 'I love the Lord, because he hath heard my voice' (Psalm 116:1). There is a great depth to the humble sufferings of Christ as the Redeemer of God's elect shining forth from Psalm 116. Let us never forget that Jesus of Nazareth, the Son of God who is also the Son of Man, took every word of every Psalm upon His own lips. Consequently when we praise God with the Psalms we are using the very same words that Christ Himself used.

As to prayer, the Gospels of Matthew, Mark, Luke and John reveal that Jesus was much given to prayer (Matthew 14:23, 26:36; Mark 1:35, 6:46, 14:32; Luke 5:16, 6:12, 9:28-29 and John 17). Nevertheless, apart from John 17 and Matthew 26, very little of Christ's prayers are recorded in the Gospels. However, David the sweet psalmist of Israel and others were used by the Holy Spirit as prophets to pen Christ's prayers! The pleadings of the Psalms are really the pleadings of Christ to His Father. These Psalms provide a deep insight and bring us to 'comprehend with all saints what *is* the breadth, and length, and depth, and height; and to know the love of Christ' (Ephesians 3:18-19).

The Judging Christ

Now, in considering the prayers of Christ in the Psalms, I trust it is not wrong to go a step further. Because Christ is the second person of the Godhead, he can plead to His Father for things which we cannot. Only Christ – who is perfectly holy – can plead for the righteous judgement of God upon the wicked. In Psalm 59:13 he pleads 'Consume *them* in wrath, consume *them*, that they *may* not *be*'. As fallen creatures, there could be sin if we were to plead such things. It is safer for us to plead, 'Thy will be done in earth, as *it is* in heaven' (Matthew 6:10).

Christ is at the centre of every Psalm and is in them from beginning to end. From Psalm 1 to Psalm 150, we are in Holy Scripture for our learning to see Christ humbling Himself, Christ suffering, Christ praying, Christ praising, Christ judging, Christ teaching as well as Christ crucified, risen and exalted. Herein is the key to our praise, that we might be drawn closer to Christ more and more, 'that I may know him, and the power of his resurrection, and the fellowship of his sufferings' (Philippians 3:10).

Concluding Warning

Finally, we need to recognise that the Devil knows that the Psalms direct us to Christ. This the Devil hates, and he will do his utmost to change and diminish the declaration of Christ as the Son of God, the Saviour of sinners. This is brought to our attention when the devil misquotes Psalm 91, verses 11-12 – which is a prophecy of Christ – during the temptations in the wilderness (Matthew 4:6). In his reference to the Psalm, the Devil removes the all-important statement, 'to keep thee in all thy ways.'

This kind of thing is a real danger in our day when men are attempting to detract from the Psalms or to remove them from the worship of God. We ought to discern the work of Satan behind such attempts. We would do well to remember that the book of Psalms is an integral part of Holy Scripture: 'Every word of God *is* pure' (Proverbs 30:5) and 'All scripture *is* given by inspiration of God, and *is* profitable for doctrine, for reproof, for correction, for instruction in righteousness: that the man of God may be perfect, thoroughly furnished unto all good works' (2 Timothy 3:16).

In this respect, Christ, in teaching His disciples, encourages them by saying to them: 'I will hear what God the Lord will speak: for he will speak peace unto his people, and to his saints: but let them not turn again to folly' (Psalm 85:8). What a blessing – and what a warning!

I trust that these few comments from a struggling soul may be of some help. It is only the Holy Spirit that can confirm truth.

Donald Balfour is a teacher of Geography and Support for Learning at Fortrose Academy, and is a member of the Dornoch congregation of the Free Presbyterian Church of Scotland.

Songs of the Spirit

IV.

The Praise of the Sanctuary
Psalms, Hymns, Paraphrases –
Their Value as Praise

William Mackay

Discussions on the subject of praise often turn upon the question of whether inspired or uninspired matter should be used. The arguments frequently come down to the practice of accredited Christians, and great names may be quoted on either side. It seems an unsatisfactory basis upon which to decide so important an issue, and I have therefore endeavoured to collect guidance from Scripture itself.

I. PSALMS
Old Testament Song

We may usefully begin by examining the development of song in the Old Testament. The first song is probably that of Lamech in Genesis 4:23-24, and is a war song. Many of the oracles of the Old Testament are cast in poetic form, e.g., the blessing of Jacob, but the first real song of praise is the Song of Moses after the crossing of the Red Sea. Then there is 32nd chapter of Deuteronomy, which God instructed Moses to teach to Israel, a song of witness against them in unfaithfulness. There follows the blessing of Moses, and the 90th Psalm is his. Then we have the songs of Deborah and of Hannah, and this brings us down to the time of David. Most of the Psalms are his, but his lament for Jonathan, and the last words of David, appear only in 2 Samuel. One of David's songs appears twice, in 2 Samuel 22, and as the 18th Psalm.

Now here we have a question which completely transcends that referred to earlier as between inspired and uninspired song. Here are songs, some of which are genuinely inspired, yet when the books of Psalms were compiled they were not included. Surely we might have expected that the song of deliverance from Egypt – the birth-song of the nation of Israel, would have a prominent place in their hymnody. Yet it is absent, along with the one which God said should not be forgotten out of the mouth of their seed. If we look at a modern hymnary we see that every song which by any stretch can be called spiritual, whatever the credentials of the writer, has been pressed into service. If these methods had operated in the case of the Psalms, then all the songs of Moses and David, with those of Deborah and Hannah, would surely have been included. How comes it that they have been omitted?

Principles of Psalm Selection
The words heading so many Psalms, 'To the Chief Musician', indicate the authorisation of psalms for use in worship. Can we discover any principles which appear to operate in the selection? I think we can. I suggest three.

1. The atmosphere of the Psalms is praise and exaltation of God, in his being, wisdom, power, holiness, justice, goodness and truth; in his word and in his works, in creation, providence, redemption. One hundred and forty-four psalms begin with God; 24 mention God in every verse. But even when the psalmist is being most personal, it is God's dealings with him which are exalted. Cf. Psalm 23; 'me' in every verse, but no egotism. What God has done is the theme. Praise is made up of expression, not of impression. Just as in the presence of Royalty, all eyes are turned to

the Monarch, and no back is turned in the Presence, so is the Psalmist before the face of God, and what he says is uttered in the ears of God. In praise, God is glorified and man is abased; and the first requirement of the Psalter is that God must be praised.

Every book of Scripture is to the glory of God, but in the historical books you have to traverse one chapter or many chapters of record before the Godward movement is evident. In the historical Psalms, on the other hand – 78, 105, 106 – you find this Godward glance rarely delayed more than two verses, and commonly in every verse.

"In praise, God is glorified and man is abased; and the first requirement of the Psalter is that God must be praised"

2. In the second place, there is a principle followed that only songs which are suitable for use in praise by all people are included among the Psalms. This does not mean that there will be no references to Jewish matters, for the Jewish economy was a typical one, and its history brings out God's purpose and government in a way which is basic for the Christian dispensation. But it does mean that the Psalms were not compiled merely or primarily as a manual of praise for the Jewish nation. Had they so been, the two songs of Moses could not possibly have been omitted. Although the Song of Exodus 15 is not included as a whole, seven psalms refer to the dividing of the sea, and 18 contain passages parallel to Deuteronomy 32. The Song of Deborah is of significance mainly for Israel, and is excluded, but a phrase of it, 'Lead thy captivity captive', appears in Psalm 68. The Song of Hannah is excluded,

but one portion of it is reproduced in Psalm 113:7-8, and every verse of it is quoted elsewhere. David's lament for Jonathan is not included – it is not praise of God, and appears to be one of the merely human and uninspired utterances of David. David's last words are not included, although inspired, being personal to himself.

We conclude then that songs which were truly national songs of Israel were not included, but only such songs as were in a form suitable to be the substance of praise to God for wider use, and by other nations.

3. In about half of the Psalms the utterance is that of a single person, and the third principle which we can trace is that this is a representative person. In some 12 of these personal Psalms, there speaks a representative sinner, David or Asaph, a saved sinner. In over 60 Psalms we have a speaker who far transcends David or Asaph in his person and character and work. He offers to God the praise of a righteous heart, but at the same time he bears a load of guilt. He is the Redeemer, and the main Psalms of this nature have been gathered by our Lord to himself, and He has said: 'It is written of Me in their Law'. The apostles have followed Christ in this teaching, and have pointed to passages which are untrue of David, and do not apply to him.

Personal Psalms Messianic

The early church appears to have consistently regarded the personal Psalms as mainly Messianic, and so did Augustine. In more modern times we have the commentaries of Bishop Home and John Brown and Andrew Bonar following the same line. It is a misfortune that Calvin in his Psalms has persisted in identifying every personal Psalm as referring in the first place to its writer, and only in a secondary way and by accommodation to Christ – even the 16th, 22nd, 40th and 69th, which are attributed solely to Christ in the New Testament. The respect in which Calvin is held as a commentator perhaps explains why in the pulpits of a Psalm-singing church such as ours, the emphasis on the primary

Messianic character of more than just a few Psalms is not more strongly made. In his commentary on Acts, written later than that on Psalms, Calvin expounds in a primary Messianic sense the same Psalms which he had treated previously as primarily referring to David. This shows that he had second thoughts, and in this case second thoughts were undoubtedly best.

We see then that David, or Asaph, as a repentant sinner was fitted under the guidance of the Spirit, to be our personal guide in that sphere. But to lead us in the way of righteousness, not simply to point it out to us, David must give place to Christ. There are two tremendous advantages in this. In the first place, our model is perfect; and in the second place, where our experience limps as we attempt to follow in his steps, our faith comes into exercise, and so we are never singing an alien, unrelated, unprescribed experience as in many hymns.

The Psalms were from the beginning divinely designed to be the vehicle of praise for all nations and generations, and not simply for the Jews. The life, death and resurrection of Christ, and his own teaching as to what the Psalms testified in regard to these matters, threw new light on the Psalms and made the book doubly acceptable as the manual of Christian praise. No new book of praise was provided. In all the abundant provision for the infant church, in the rich gifts – wisdom, knowledge, faith, healing, miracles, prophecy, discernment, tongues, interpretation (1 Corinthians 12:8) – showered upon its members, in the various offices – apostles, prophets, teachers, and so on – by which it was served, there is not the breath of a suggestion that a new psalmody was necessary, or that a new psalmist was being appointed.

The hymn-book of the Christian Church was completed hundreds of years before, and needed only the resurrection and ascension of Christ to interpret it, because in the Psalms Christ is always viewed from the post-advent standpoint. The practice of the apostolic church completely confirms this assertion, and the early church followed apostolic practice.

II. HYMNS

"The most unexceptionable of hymns gathered into one collection strike one immediately by this characteristic of having man central and God accessory"

The first competitors to take the field against the Psalms were those hymns which appeared in the second century to promote Gnostic and similar heresies. The 'hymns and spiritual songs', on the other hand, mentioned in Ephesians and Colossians, are terms used in the Septuagint to describe Psalms, and the hymn mentioned in Matthew is also a Psalm. Some of the Gnostic hymns praised practical graces, and were very popular. The orthodox party wrote counter hymns, but they did not take well because they were mostly credal and lacking in warmth. Then later followed the Greek and Latin hymns, contemplative, narrative, subjective, which set the fashion for modern hymnody.

Many hymns are an expression of the Christian experience, sentiments, ambitions, prayers of the writer, and have many of the valuable characteristics of a Christian diary. Diaries such as those of Boston, Fraser, Halyburton and Bonar can be profitable reading for other Christians. In the same way, hymns like Murray McCheyne's 'I once was a stranger', or Charlotte Elliott's 'Just as I am', describe the writer's conversion in a simple and moving way, calculated to help others to take the same path. But they are of necessity subjective compositions, not possessing the high characteristics of praise as exemplified in the Psalms, and not in fact written with such an end in view. It is no offence to be subjective – the book of Job for example is almost entirely so. We have nothing but respect for such hymns. But we do have a quarrel with those who collected such hymns and submitted them as a substitute for the divine manual. The most unexceptionable of hymns gathered into one collection strike one immediately by this characteristic of having man central and God accessory.

Murray McCheyne, whom we have quoted, would have viewed with abhorrence the idea of using any composition of his as a substitute for the Psalms in public praise. But there were many hymn-writers who thought that God had left Himself without a witness in the matter of praise in New Testament times, and that it was incumbent upon them to supply the deficiency. Isaac Watts rewrote the psalms to make David speak like a Christian, and other hymn-writers have adopted equally presumptuous roles. The results can only be described as disastrous. I propose to summarise briefly some of these.

Defects in Hymns

1. The vast majority of hymns have an overwhelmingly subjective note, even when the matter of many individual hymns is good. A writer in support of hymns says: 'The true hymn must have a motion Godward. It is not exactly necessary that God should be directly addressed, but God must be uppermost in the thought if not particularly conspicuous in the expression. The true hymn must tend towards God; bring him to mind; exalt his name, and seek his glory. Those which are simply introspective, didactic, dogmatic, sentimental, egotistical, and the like are not hymns. Some so-called hymns are like the Pharisee's utterances in the temple, they do not contain a single element of praise.' In my view, the vast majority of hymns fail to reach the standard here laid down.

2. In hymns generally, God is contemplated as almost always friendly, the sinner being righteous. The prevalence of wickedness, and God's judgment of it, upon which an equal emphasis is laid in the psalms, is almost ignored.

3. The prophetic portions of praise regarding the life, death,

resurrection and rule of Christ are lost altogether in hymns.

4. There are hosts of positive errors of which only some of the more general can be noticed. In his attempt to be vivid the hymnist often succeeds only in being superficial. A striking example of this can be seen in the employment of the word 'cross'. This is a word whose use can be seen to change under our very eyes in the New Testament. Before the death of Christ, the word cross meant the wooden stake on which a condemned man under Roman rule was exposed to die. After Christ rose we do not find the word cross thus used. The word 'tree' is substituted five times. The apostle Paul, taught by the Spirit of God to adapt spiritual words to spiritual truths, used the word cross as equivalent to atonement by the vicarious death of Christ. When he preached the cross and gloried in the cross, it is not the mere wood or symbol that is in question. Even in the one case where at first glance the use might appear to be literal – 'blotting out the hand-writing of ordinances, nailing it to his cross', (Colossians 2:14) – the action is figurative, and can be explained only in terms of the complete atonement.

The cross symbol is not found until the fourth century. The Emperor Constantine modified the heathen sistrum of Osiris to make an emblem behind which both heathen and Christian could march. The Roman Church, with its veneration of the 'true cross', its 'crusades' and crucifixes, perpetuated the error and the Anglican Church retained it, signing children in baptism with the sign of the cross, and multiplying the symbol within and without its churches. The Reformed Churches cast out this symbol and use of a cross as pagan, but in the hymnary we have it reintroduced in force, substituting the weak and beggarly element for the vital spiritual truth. For example:

> *With the cross of Jesus going on before* – S. Gould
> *When I survey the wondrous cross* – Watts
> *Hold Thou thy cross before my closing eyes* – Lyte
> *Simply to thy cross I cling* – Toplady
> *Beneath the cross of Jesus* – Clephane

The old rugged cross – Bennard.

Almost every reference in hymns is capable of being interpreted mainly of the physical cross. The cross in the Pauline sense you can find in the 22nd, 40th, 96th and 102nd Psalms, where you have one who claims perfect righteousness bearing and confessing a load of guilt. The degradation of the word 'cross' has been greatly fostered by the use of hymns, and the Biblical doctrine of atonement has become an offence.

When people set out to compile a hymnary it is evident that a very large charity possesses them – to every sort of composition except the Psalms. The doubts of Arthur Hugh Clough, in 'Say not the struggle not availeth' do not exclude him, nor the defection of John Henry Newman. In the latter's hymn 'Lead kindly light', there are two manifest improprieties which should put us immediately on our guard. In the first place God is not to be addressed as one of his attributes. He is a personal God, who covers himself with light. In the second place there is no light in Scripture with the characteristics which Newman gives to it. There is the light to which he that doeth truth approaches; there is the light to your path, which you carry with you; and there is the light of dawn which shines more and more unto the perfect day. Newman's light, which led him on o'er moore and fen, is the spiritual counterpart of the will-o'-the-wisp which landed him in the bog of Romanism.

In Bridge's 'Crown him with many crowns' you have a vain intrusion into things unseen, with Christ walking in a flowery pagan meadow and hailed as the fruit of the 'Mystic Rose', – the Virgin Mary, and the writer stage-managing the heavenly attendants.

Nature imagery is very largely used, the waves roll high and the winds sweep by. Cloud and sunshine, crag and torrent, stormy seas and shady rills, pad out their vague and uncertain story, to create an atmosphere without commitment. There is a difference between a wish and a prayer. Balaam said: 'Let me die the death of the righteous, and let my last end be his'. That was a wish. Balaam loved the wages of unrighteousness, but wished for the righteous man's reward. The hymns are full of wishes and sighs, and as substitutes for prayer for the realities they are dangerous things. Wishful thinking, instead of prayerful seeking, is a form of 'sweet, sweet, sweet poison for the age's tooth'. The 'Christian Year' promotes observance of feasts devised by men out of their own hearts, and substitutes a subtle but appealing form of ritualism for the sacraments and Sabbaths of Christ's appointment.

I have been struck on turning the pages of a Spiritualist hymn book to find out how many popular hymns they have been able to incorporate with little or no alteration in their manual. Those hymns in which invocation is made to light, to joy, to love, instead of to a personal God, lend themselves readily to such a transfer. There were only two Psalm portions to be found in the book.

We may ask ourselves in what attitude we should approach God. The Psalmist does so with a godly fear, with love mixed with reverence. The Lord Jesus in His earthly life was gentle and patient with His disciples, yet there was always deep respect in their address. After His resurrection, this reverence is even more pronounced. And when He appeared to John in Patmos, it was with a glory which caused the beloved and loving disciple to fall at his feet as dead. God has been pleased to make himself familiar to his chosen ones such as Abraham and Moses and Daniel, but we never read of them seeking to presume by treating God in an offhand way. Yet one of the chief ways in which some hymn-writers have lost touch with spiritual reality is in their over-familiar approach. There are hymns which achieve consecration of their writers only at the expense of the desecration of their Lord.

Doctrinal Errors in Hymns

In a typical hymnary I find that there are not more than one third of the hymns from which there do not leap up objections on the ground of bad doctrine, irreverence, pride, or complacency. The inoffensive remnant is so preponderantly experimental or didactive, so as to lack the characteristics of praise; as the Psalms have taught us to interpret it.

The effect of the doctrinal and other errors of hymnaries is far more powerful than is commonly realised. If we are taught nothing but truth, it is still the case that as fallible creatures we succeed in infusing our own error into it. Did not our Lord tell His disciples over and over again that He had come to die? But they persisted in their own belief that He had come to reign. Calvin says, 'Such is the proneness of the human mind to go astray, that it will more quickly draw error from one little word, than truth from a lengthy discourse'. Even under our Lord's perfect teaching, men picked up errors. But mix with your truth a mere 5 per cent of error and what do you find? That small modicum of error has become almost the whole content of the hearer's assimilation.

"For people not diligent in the study of Scripture, the hymn, imprinted in the memory by rhythm and melody, is the more effective teaching agency, and its wrong standards act as an antidote to truth"

There is selective absorption of the wrong element. For people not diligent in the study of Scripture, the hymn, imprinted in the memory by rhythm and melody, is the more effective teaching agency, and its wrong standards act as an antidote to truth. All that was said in a recent *Monthly Record* about the shift of emphasis from knowledge to feeling in Modernism applies equally to hymn collections, without which Modernism would be deprived of one of its most effective buttresses.

I know of no Church using hymns which does not have a deep cleavage within it in regard to matters of faith or practice. This is no accident. A converted person grounded in Scripture has an antidote to the influence of hymns which often enables him to appear to suffer little adverse effect. An unconverted person lacks this antidote, and the hymns, by their doubtful expressions, and omissions of vital truth, as much as by their positive errors, confirm him in his natural disposition.

Hymns are also great dividers between churches, because from Gnostic times right up to the present day each difference of belief prefers to be fortified by its own particular hymnody.

The Psalms, divinely accredited as the vehicle of praise, are calculated to be a unifying influence with such as regard the sovereignty of God and the authority of Scripture. That is another reason why we should be militant in our advocacy of their use.

III. PARAPHRASES

Now a word about paraphrases. What is a paraphrase? The metrical Psalms were formerly called metrical paraphrases of the Psalms. The prose Psalm says, 'The Lord is my shepherd; I shall not want. He maketh me to lie down in green pastures'; and the metrical paraphrase says, 'The Lord's my shepherd, I'll not want. He makes me down to lie'. That is, the metrical paraphrase says the same thing as the prose, but the words are rearranged to fall into metre with as little change as possible. The first thing therefore to note about the so-called paraphrases is that one-third of them are not paraphrases at all, and another third are loose transcripts. Some verses are good renderings of Scriptures; for example, the paraphrase of Romans 3:19-20: 'No hope can on the law be built', etc. But, 'Ye indolent and slothful! Rise, view the ant's labours and be wise', lacks the terse homeliness of the original. Neither of these, however, is praise, but rather preaching and exhortation, spoken from God to man, not man to God.

In Genesis 28 we have, 'And Jacob awakened', etc., and in the 2nd paraphrase, 'O God of Bethel'. This is of course no paraphrase, but just a hymn based on a thought suggested by the prose passage. We must not be misled by a name.

The majority of the so-called paraphrases take quite

unwarranted liberties with their material, padding out the divine word with human concepts. There is no virtue in turning aside from what God has appointed for singing, and putting in its place what God has appointed to be preached or narrated. There may be good reason with an illiterate people for using the metrical form in narrative to aid the memory. The *Gude and Godly Ballads* in Scotland, and Luther's hymns in Germany, greatly helped the spread of the Reformation. But we must not fall under the delusion that because something is in verse, it thereby becomes automatically praise, as collectors of hymnody have been so prone to imagine.

If I were briefed to get an orthodox, Psalm-singing church off the Scriptures, I should suggest first that they be induced to use the paraphrases, as being the word of God in verse. After a generation or so, I should point out to them that there are hymns (like 'Rock of Ages') even more Scriptural than some paraphrases (such as 'O God of Bethel'), and get them to adopt a few of the better hymns. After that one might do as occasion served to get the hymns up to 500 to displace both paraphrases and Psalms. This is not really very original – it happened like that in our own Church. In the 1870s the General Assembly of the Free Church of Scotland agreed to admit 'twenty-five hymns of the better sort'. In a matter of ten years there were hundreds, and they played an important part in the downgrade movement in spiritual things towards the close of last century.

CONCLUSION

The difference between the proudest composition of uninspired man, attempting to reveal God, and the humblest Psalm, is all the way between earth and heaven. In the Psalms we have Scripture in miniature – history, biography, theology, prophecy, devotion – all clothed in the garment of praise, and expressed, as regards many of them, through the lips of a mediator, of whose thoughts they are largely composed. Hymnaries by comparison, in what they include, and still more in what they are unable to express, are but as the chaff to the wheat.

> God's law is perfect and converts
> > the soul in sin that lies:
> God's testimony is most sure,
> > and makes the simple wise.

It is our privilege as well as our wisdom to witness to ourselves and others that this evangelistic missionary's vitalising message is no less that of the Psalms than of the Gospels or any other books, a truth that many have forgotten.

Chapter IV was originally an Address delivered to the Annual Reunion of the Free Church Students' Association and was printed in the Monthly Record of the Free Church of Scotland, *April 1956, 67-71.*

Major William Morton Mackay, M.C., fought as an Army officer in both World Wars, lectured in Electrical Engineering at the University of St Andrews, and served for many years as a ruling elder in the Dundee congregation of the Free Church of Scotland. He died in 1971.

V.

Sing the Lord's Song
Biblical Psalms in Worship

John Keddie

I. SETTING THE SCENE

The singing of praise to the Lord has been a feature of Church life from Old Testament times. Before even the specifications of the Tabernacle were revealed, there was an outpouring of inspired song to the Lord. The Exodus from Egypt drew out the Song of Moses (Exodus 15:1-18) and the Song of Miriam:

> 'Sing to the LORD,
> For He has triumphed gloriously!
> The horse and its rider
> He has thrown into the sea' (Exodus 15:21).

Through to the last book of the New Testament the redeemed of the Lord have a song to sing in His praise. Indeed, the song of the redeemed in glory is the song of Moses and the song of the Lamb (Revelation 15:3-4). In this way a link is forged between the first inspired song of Scripture and the last! It can readily be recognized that song has always played an important part in the life of the Church of the Living God.

The position of Psalms in worship

Until relatively recently the inspired Psalms of Scripture enjoyed a position of prominence in the praises of the Church. These Songs of Zion in one form or another have encouraged, uplifted, instructed and inspired generations of earnest Christians. The Reformation of the sixteenth century saw a renewal in congregational Psalm singing, restoring a practice which prevailed in the early Church. Subsequently, especially in Presbyterian Churches, Metrical Psalms were more or less exclusively used in services of public worship.

Today the situation is very different. The Psalms of Scripture have been largely displaced in modern Church worship. Patterns of worship are changing with baffling rapidity. Songs and hymns entirely of man's devising and composition have proliferated. It appears that anything goes in today's worship, in which there is a constant desire for something new. Worship services and evangelistic programs devote a significant amount of time to hymn and chorus singing. The Psalms of Holy Scripture seem to have been left well behind. Churches which have maintained Psalm singing are under pressure to change on the grounds that such praise today is regarded as a hindrance to people coming in to the Church. Perhaps such praise may even be considered as 'restrictive' by some, or as not encouraging 'real' worship.

The situation in worship today

In all this flux in the area of the public worship of God it is easier to recognize what men desire or demand than to establish Biblical answers to such questions as: 'What does the Lord warrant in His worship?' 'Is the Bible not clear on what we are to use in worship?' 'Do we really have to rely upon what is "modern," however that is to be measured, or by whomever it is to be determined?'

To some degree it will be unavoidable that the style of a people's music will be moulded by cultural factors. But will that be true also of the content? Has the Lord not provided a manual of praise? It is to such considerations that this chapter is devoted. The basic thesis is that reformation is widely needed in this area of worship. It is maintained that a return requires to be made both to a responsible and God-centred 'regulative principle' of worship in general, and, in particular, to the use in sung praise of materials of God's inspiration and appointment.

A case for using only inspired materials of praise

It is a concern of this chapter to establish that in the area of public worship there

> "It is a concern of this chapter to establish that in the area of public worship there is warrant for the use in congregational song only of materials of direct divine inspiration"

is warrant for the use in congregational song only of materials of direct divine inspiration. By 'materials of direct divine inspiration' is meant those writings which derive their content, thought, detail, truth and authority from the fact that they are the Word of God written, and are part of the canon of Holy Scripture, infallibly and inerrantly produced under the inspiration of the Spirit of God (cf. Hebrews 1:1; 2 Peter 1:21; 2 Timothy 3:16). In other words, presupposed in this study is a high doctrine of Scripture and of the canon of Holy Scripture, as expressed for example in the *Westminster Confession of Faith*, Chapter 1.

By 'uninspired' is meant all writings not part of the canon of Holy Scripture, however true to the Scriptures they may seem to be. It is our conviction that there is warrant for the use of the Book of Psalms in sung praise in the public worship of God. But what about other songs found in Scripture outside the Psalter?

The status of songs outside the Psalter

On the face of it, the use of other songs in Scripture outside the Psalter does not seem objectionable as the principle of advocating only inspired song is not violated. Yet our concern should be to use only what has divine sanction and approval. There is clear sanction for the Book of Psalms. Such sanction is not clear in connection with other songs found in Scripture. These may have been intended for a more temporary or personal or national use, and in any case scarcely express truths not already found in the Psalms. On this question the conclusion of John Murray in his *Minority Report of the Committee on Song in the Public Worship of God*, presented to the General Assembly of the Orthodox Presbyterian Church in 1947, commends itself: 'In view of the uncertainty with respect to the use of other inspired songs, we should confine ourselves to the Book of Psalms.'

The question of Scripture Paraphrases

It is granted that even within the Reformed tradition Bible materials other than the 150 Psalms, such as Scripture Paraphrases, have been used occasionally in Psalm-singing Churches. To this writer there are two main objections to the adoption of such materials. *(1) There is no clear warrant in Scripture for putting into verse for singing parts of the Bible not originally recorded in the form of song; and (2) it is rather presumptuous for any person or group of people to take upon themselves the responsibility for selecting passages to be adapted for singing.* After all, if the Lord has not caused such passages to be expressed in the form of songs nor indicated that such passages should be paraphrased for singing, by what authority do men take on this responsibility?

A personal reflection

Perhaps at this point a personal comment may be in order. The writer was brought up in a mainstream Presbyterian hymn singing tradition. Little thought was given, as it happens, either to the content of the hymns or the principles, if any, behind their selection as materials for praise in the Church. That is not to say that the singers did not mean what they sang, or that care was not taken in their selection. But the principle of hymn singing - of the use of uninspired materials for praise - was not questioned. It was just accepted, no questions asked. Good men must have agreed this. That was good enough for me, and no doubt also for most other people. However, when I came to realize that for the greater part the Churches of the Reformation used only the Psalms of Scripture, and likewise the English Puritans and Scottish Covenanters, not to speak of most eighteenth- and nineteenth-century Presbyterians in Britain, in the Dominions and in the United States of America, I began to question my hitherto unthinking acceptance of modern hymnals. I began to ask: 'Is there not, after all, at least a good argument for using only the God-breathed songs of Holy Scripture in the formal public praises of the Lord?'

The discovery and study of some expositions of this position, mostly from the nineteenth century, did nothing to quell my newfound uncertainties on this question. Indeed, in the process of time I became convinced of the 'regulative principle,' that only what is sanctioned by God in His Word is appropriate in public worship. It was then a short step to the position adopted by almost all evangelical Christian Churches at some time in their past, that in the Psalms of Scripture there is a satisfactory and sufficient manual of praise even for the Christian Church. As I became more familiar with the Psalms, I came to see their richness in spiritual experience; their perfect theological balance; the reality that Christ is in all the Psalms as He is in 'all the Scriptures' (cf. Luke 24:44). The Psalms, I came to see, tend to produce a distinctive type of piety that is thoroughly God-centred and experiential in a balanced way, as one would expect from using materials of divine inspiration. I was convinced.

This is not to say that a Psalm-singing Church is, consequently, a perfect Church. It is not to say that its performance of praise cannot be improved or, for that matter, that the *translations*

"The practice of congregational Psalm singing was itself once widespread, at least in the Reformed Churches. A review of modern hymnals reveals just how the praise materials of the modern Church largely date from the late eighteenth century"

of the Psalms sung may not be revised and improved periodically. But at least it does mean that one can have perfect confidence, using only songs of divine revelation, that one is always singing in public worship songs of which the Lord wholly approves, something that cannot be said even of what may be considered the best of human compositions.

II. FREQUENTLY ASKED QUESTIONS

In addressing the issue of what materials are appropriate vehicles for praise in the Christian Church many questions arise in people's minds, especially when the predominant position on the use of uninspired materials is questioned. At this point we will deal with some possible problems or misunderstandings that arise, or objections that are often raised against confining the praise materials to Biblical Psalms.

Isn't this just a minority opinion?

Someone might say: 'This is a minority opinion nowadays. There must therefore be a presumption against this view. The vast majority of Christians surely can't be wrong.' What can one say about this argument? Obviously there is no special virtue in holding a minority opinion. By the same token, however, minority opinion or practice is not necessarily wrong. It was a majority opinion in

Israel that there should be a king to rule. Yet that did not seem to be right in God's eyes, nor good for the nation in the longer term (see 1 Samuel 8:1-22; 10:17-27; 15:10-35)! Majority opinion in Church history has often occasioned oppression or even tyranny. Majority opinion itself, therefore, and likewise any minority view, is to be subjected to the overriding consideration: What does God say? What is Scriptural (cf. Romans 4:3: Galatians 4:30)?

The truth is that Old Testament prophets and New Testament apostles were often called to counter majority opinion or practice. Mention of the prophet Jeremiah is sufficient to prove this point. Again and again these men found themselves in a minority and frequently seemed to be standing alone for the claims of truth. Even the Lord Jesus Christ in His days on earth did not command majority support. Yet He was completely right. We should not make too much of where the majority stand. Nor should a minority practice be discounted simply because it has little support. At the same time it has to be said that the practice of congregational Psalm singing was itself once widespread, at least in the Reformed Churches. A review of modern hymnals reveals just how the praise materials of the modern Church largely date from the late eighteenth century. Whatever else may be said of this it is clear that by and large the praise materials of the majority of Churches today are neither apostolic in origin nor specifically commanded by God in his Word. In our estimation this raises serious questions for the modern hymn singer.

Were the hymn writers all wrong?

This question may then be raised: 'Are you saying that all these hymn writers, whose hymns have been so signally blessed, were wrong and out of step with the Lord?' The answer to this is an emphatic 'No!' The argument is *not* about whether it was right or wrong for this or that person to compose hymns and religious songs. It is not disputed that there are many hymns of quite exceptional poetic quality, doctrinal soundness and devotional sweetness. It is not disputed that hymns have been greatly blessed to many souls over the years. What is questioned is the warrant to use such hymns and songs of merely human composition in the formal and public worship of the Church. Although such compositions may contain excellent sentiments even the best of them fall short of being immediately inspired by God. In this connection 'inspired' refers specifically to what is canonical Scripture. It is true that some people will say that this or that hymn writer has surely been 'inspired' and has produced inspiring song. In a sense that may be correct, but not in the sense that there has been divine inspiration, an inspiration attributable only to the writers of the Holy Scriptures. This is a far more significant point than is usually admitted.

What about the question of blessing?

'If Psalm singing is so right, why aren't Churches maintaining that position more obviously blessed'? The matter of the praise materials of a Church is only one aspect of that Church's responsiveness to the Lord. There are many other important aspects of a Church's life and witness in which there must be obedience to the word and will of the Lord. Blessing will certainly be hindered where people or a Church fail to obey the Lord. Care has to be taken in claiming a particular cause and effect in the matter of blessing enjoyed within a Church or denomination. What can be said is that there is a relationship between the Lord's blessing and a people's faithfulness. We see this reflected, for example, in the call of Abraham (Genesis 12:1-3), when the Lord tells him to move to another land and adds a promise of blessing for himself and for the world as he responds to this call. But we have to be cautious here. For it may be that whilst a remnant is faithful, the Lord's displeasure against a generation is such that He refuses to bless, despite the presence of a Noah or a Daniel or a Job (cf. Ezekiel 14:12ff).

It can be maintained that the Church has enjoyed blessing and revival in periods when only Biblical Psalms were used in praise. A Psalm-singing Church will not lack the blessing of the

Lord because it confines its praise materials to the Biblical Psalms. Lack of blessing in any Church will arise from disobedience somewhere in the work and outlook of that Church, perhaps even on account of a doctrinally diffuse and devotionally unbalanced hymnody.

Isn't this an unnecessarily divisive issue?
'Are there not far more important issues to be concerned about than arguing about psalms and hymns?' There is no doubt that there are other matters of serious and far-reaching importance confronting the Church. It is undeniably a priority within the Church to present the gospel to sinners that they might be saved and avoid a lost eternity. Mission must be in the forefront of the Church's task in the world: 'Go therefore and make disciples of all the nations, baptizing them in the name of the Father and of the Son and of the Holy Spirit' (Matthew 28:19). But, of course, there is more. The Great Commission itself does not end there. Jesus goes on to say: 'teaching them to observe all things that I have commanded you; and lo, I am with you always, even to the end of the age' (v.20). The Church is charged not only to evangelize, but also to instruct; to keep the word of Christ; to conform to His teaching and not, knowingly and willingly, to step beyond it, however much people may consider themselves competent to add to or improve upon what is there.

Is this not a relatively unimportant matter?
Whenever the question of the content of the Church's praise is raised it is not uncommon for people to suggest that it is a secondary matter. But is that right? The truth is that the great priority of the Christian Church in the broadest sense is the worship of God. What could be more important? Is it not the case that the order of the Church's priorities is this: first of all, the worship of God; secondly, the building up of the body of Christ; and thirdly, the proclamation of the gospel to those outside? These of course must all be found in a living Church or congregation. But it stands to

reason that if the first two elements mentioned are not right then there will be little effectiveness in the third. At the same time as it calls sinners to come faith in Jesus Christ, the gospel is calling people back to the true worship of God (cf. Revelation 14:6-7). In view of this it is a mistake to reckon the content of praise a matter, relatively speaking, of indifference for the confessing Church.

It is also common for people to maintain that there is a hierarchy of priorities in the Scriptures. Some feel, for instance, that the demands of evangelism take precedence over such concerns as the principles or practices of worship. It is true no doubt that there are some things relatively more important than others in the life of the Christian Church as it is guided by the Word of God. But it is a mistake to think that there are demands in the Word of God so relatively unimportant that we can dispense with them, as if we can put aside certain things simply because we perceive them to be not so important in the Church's work or witness. It is dangerous for mere men to decide which parts of Scripture are necessary and sufficient, and which we can safely ignore or treat as relatively indifferent. It is for the Church, rather, to come *under* the teaching of Scripture as fully sufficient in all matters of faith *and* practice (cf. 2 Timothy 3:14-17). As the *Westminster Larger Catechism* puts it, in answer to the question, 'What is the word of God?' (Q3): 'The holy scriptures of the Old and New Testament are the word of God, the only rule of faith and obedience.' The *Confession of Faith* is explicit on this: 'The whole counsel of God concerning all things necessary for His own glory, man's salvation, faith and life, is either expressly set down in Scripture, or by good and necessary consequence may be deduced from Scripture: unto which nothing at any time is to be added, whether by new revelations of the Spirit or traditions of men' (I:6).

It is all too easy to say that the matter of the specific praise materials is not central or foremost in the Church's concerns. Yet the Holy Scriptures contain a Book of 150 Psalms, clearly intended for praise among the people of God. It is an irony, no doubt, that in modern patterns of worship the praise element does tends to loom large as a matter of considerable significance. Nowadays worship services are increasingly taken up with praise and singing, and decreasingly with the proclamation of God's word. In all this people are being asked to engage in the worship of God! The words that are being taken on people's lips ought to be pleasing to the Lord. That must, therefore, be a central concern. Consequently, it is important to enquire about the sufficiency of Scripture in the matter. Jesus put the Church's task in proper perspective when He said in the parable of the unjust steward that 'he who is faithful in what is least is faithful also in much; and he who is unjust in what is least, is unjust also in much' (Luke 16:10).

> "It is all too easy to say that the matter of the specific praise materials is not central or foremost in the Church's concerns. Yet the Holy Scriptures contain a Book of 150 Psalms, clearly intended for praise among the people of God"

Isn't this a matter of the heart?

Someone may object: 'Does it matter so much what we're singing as long as it is not positively unsound? Isn't it the spirit that is important and not the letter?' There is some plausibility in this argument. Dead formalism in singing even the best materials is scarcely superior to singing with spiritual fervor songs not drawn from the Scriptures. A right attitude of worship cannot be automatically assumed simply because Bible songs are used. The Lord clearly desires the spiritual attitude expressed by the writer to the Hebrews: 'Therefore by him [i.e. by Jesus] let us continually offer the sacrifice of praise to God, that is, the fruit of our lips, giving thanks to his name' (Hebrews 13:15). The issue, however, is not the attitude of the worshipper's heart. It is not doubted that people singing hymns of merely human composition may have a good spirit of worship and a real earnestness. The issue here is this: What materials for praise does the Lord desire His Church to use? What songs unquestionably have His approval, his sanction and his seal? An example from the Bible illustrates the point, that the spirit or heart of the thing is not the only, or even the primary consideration. When Aquila and Priscilla encountered Apollos at Ephesus they found him to be a man instructed in the way of the Lord and 'fervent in spirit.' He even taught accurately the things of the Lord, though, we are told, 'he knew only the baptism of John.' So what did Aquila and Priscilla do after they heard him preaching? 'They took him aside and explained to him the way of God *more accurately.*' They did not question his sincerity or fervency or even his general soundness. But they did make good his deficiencies in Christian ordinances (Acts 18:24-28; see also Acts 19:1-7 for a similar incident involving the Apostle Paul).

Doesn't the New Testament give greater liberties in the elements of worship?

It is true that there is relatively little said in the New Testament of the precise patterns of worship. It is also true that there is a certain continuity and discontinuity between the Testaments which is not easy to define. However, are there grounds for maintaining that differences between the Old and New Testaments might allow for the adoption of elements into our worship which the Lord has not prescribed in Scripture? There are two passages of Jesus' teaching that bear powerfully on this question.

(a) First of all, in Mark 7 there is record of a debate between Jesus and the Pharisees. At issue were laws which the Pharisees superimposed upon the Biblical commandments, laws which they laid down for everybody simply on their own initiative and authority. In response Jesus quotes Isaiah 29:13: 'This people honours me with their lips, but their heart is far from me. And in vain they worship me, teaching as doctrines the commandments of men' (vv.6-7). In countering the attitudes and actions of the Pharisees, Jesus goes on to state that they were 'making the word of God of no effect' through their tradition which they had handed down - their tradition which had *no warrant from the word of God!* (v.13). 'In vain they worship me, teaching as doctrines the commandments of men.' This shows rather clearly that, (i) Jesus was aware of *continuity* in this respect at least with the Old Testament; and, (ii) for the elements of the worship of God sanction is required from the word of God. There is no scope, according to the principle stated by the Lord here, for the introduction of elements of worship simply on the initiative and authority of men.

(b) The second passage in question is in John 4 in which there is recorded a conversation between the Lord Jesus Christ and an unnamed woman at the well of Sychar in Samaria. John 4:23-24, together with Jesus' general discussion with the woman, stress the need for *inwardness* in worship. However, in the terms Jesus states here, such worship is to be consonant with the nature of God: 'the hour is coming, and now is, when the true worshippers will worship the Father in spirit and truth; for the Father is seeking such to worship him.' It must be inward, spiritual worship - from the heart; but it must also be according to truth: 'God is a Spirit, and those who worship him must worship in spirit and in truth.' It must be consistent with His revealed will rather than according to the judgments of men, points powerfully made also in Colossians 2:8-23 and Romans 1:21-25. Incidentally, in this discussion at Sychar, Jesus is clearly aware of *discontinuity* with the Old Testament, as he implies the disappearance or abrogation of the Temple and its services, including the sacrifices, the priesthood, and the musical instrumentation associated with the Temple and its worship. From this it can be maintained that in passing from the Old Testament to the New Testament, whatever discontinuity was involved, there is no evidence whatsoever that God has surrendered the right to determine acceptable worship. For the New Testament Church, too, the concern must be: What is sanctioned in the word of God?

Do you have a case?

The burden of this chapter is quite simply to put a case. We shall look in the first place at Biblical material in any way bearing on the content of praise for the New Testament Church. We shall then consider certain doctrinal and historical matters, including the question of a Biblical regulative principle

"It is our conviction, however, that a reformation is needed in this area of public worship through a return to the use of inspired Biblical song"

governing the worship of God. Hopefully, this will neither be seen as majoring on minors nor as casting any doubt on the sincerity or piety of those who by choice or simply default, sing songs other than those provided in the Holy Scriptures. It is our conviction, however, that a reformation is needed in this area of public worship through a return to the use of inspired Biblical song. No doubt there are many fine hymns, ancient and modern, and perhaps there is a place for these in the lives of the people of God. But in the place of public worship nothing should supplant what God has inspired and provided for use in His Church. It might even be said to be a scandal in the modern Church that the Psalms of Scripture have been so largely, and in some places completely, displaced by the compositions of mere men.

May the Lord lead more and more Churches and Christians to turn to the Psalms themselves as the primary source of a balanced Biblical piety and spirituality. May more and more Churches and

Christians revive the devotional use of the psalms both in private and in corporate worship. It will then be discovered that the Lord God who inspired these wonderful compositions and the Christ who is to be found spoken of throughout them, and who speaks through them Himself, may become more powerful realities in the life of God's Church.

III. THE BIBLICAL MATERIAL

Psalm Singing Commanded

Singing praise to the Lord is a distinct element in the worship of God. Naturally the question has to be asked: What does the Lord require of His Church in this regard? What has He commanded? What has He provided? Does this matter? At least in one respect there does not seem to be any doubt about what the Lord has provided and commanded in the matter of His praise. The Psalms of Scripture are to be sung by His people. There is ample evidence for this in the Psalms themselves, but also and not least, in the New Testament. Let us briefly review the evidence here:

There are the implications of the titles of the Psalms

There is no reason to believe that these titles are not of considerable antiquity and perfectly authentic. They appear to have been included with the Psalms during the time the Old Testament was in the making. Thirty-four Psalms in the Hebrew text do not have a title, though in the Septuagint (or LXX) - the Greek translation of the Old Testament which was completed about 180 B.C. - only two lack titles. Whether or not these titles are to be considered part of the original inspired text is a matter of dispute, but as Edward J. Young points out, they 'are to be regarded as trustworthy and of great value in determining the Psalm in question.' The New Testament writers would certainly have been familiar with the various Psalm titles. The fact that no fewer than 55 Psalms are addressed 'to the Chief Musician' points eloquently to the purpose of the Psalms.

There are implications from the form of the Psalms

For the greater part the poetry of the Psalms is characterized by a parallelism and rhythm of sense, rather than by the type of rhyming meters distinctive of Western poetry. However, the rhythmic structure of the Psalms was no doubt designed to be consistent with an underlying musical form. Derek Kidner explains that, 'the poetry of the Psalms has a broad simplicity of rhythm and imagery which survives transplanting into almost any soil. Above all, the fact that its parallelisms are those of sense rather than of sound allows it to reproduce its chief effects with very little loss of either force or beauty. It is well fitted by God's providence to invite "all the earth" to "sing the glory of his name".' This is a point, incidentally, which answers the problem some have with the translation of the Psalms into a metrical form for singing within our Western musical tradition.

There are the direct statements in the Psalms, and also from elsewhere in Scripture

In Psalm 95: 'Let us come before his presence with thanksgiving; let us shout joyfully to him with psalms' (v.2). In Psalm 105: 'Sing to him, sing psalms to him; talk of all his wondrous works' (v.2). Besides this, in many Psalms there is encouragement to sing to the Lord with the words of the Psalms. Such encouragement is to be found in at least 37 Psalms.

But even outside the Psalter there are clear enough indicators of the use of the Psalms by the worshippers. In 1 Chronicles 16 we find Psalms being sung when David placed the Ark of God in the Tabernacle. In Nehemiah 12, Psalms of thanksgiving were sung after the restoration and rebuilding of the walls of Jerusalem. These Psalms were led by appointed singers (see vv. 8 and 27). In the New Testament, too, there is clear encouragement to sing Psalms (cf. Ephesians 5:19; Colossians 3:16).

There are the implications of New Testament teaching

The book of Psalms is frequently cited in the New Testament. To a significant degree New Testament theology and experience are derived from the Psalms. Jesus himself claimed this. He said when He appeared to His disciples after His resurrection: 'all things must be fulfilled which were written in the Law of Moses and the Prophets and the Psalms concerning me' (Luke 24: 44). This is how it can he said with truth and conviction that Christ is in all the Scriptures. Of course Christ Himself did not just begin to exist at His conception in the womb of the virgin. He said of Himself: 'Before Abraham was, I AM' (John 8:58; cf. Colossians 1:16-18). It may be argued that some Psalms more directly and explicitly point to the Messiah or are more specifically applicable to Him. Yet, as Professor Edmund Clowney, formerly of Westminster Theological Seminary, reminds us, 'In their theological depth the psalms are songs of God's covenant and of the hope of the covenant. Since God's great work of salvation will be accomplished by the Son of David, the psalms are explicitly messianic.' Writing in 1859 Andrew Bonar was to say this about Christ in the Psalms: 'Now, in the early ages, men full of the thoughts of Christ could never read the Psalms without being reminded of the Lord. They probably had no system or fixed theory as to all the Psalms referring to Christ; but still ... they found their thoughts wandering to their Lord, as the one Person in whom these breathings, these praises, these desires, these hopes, these deep feelings, found their only true and full realization. Hence Augustine (Psalm 58) said to his hearers, as he expounded to them this book, that "the voice of Christ and his Church was well-nigh the only voice to be heard in the Psalms."'

There is no reasonable doubt that the Psalms are themselves essential Biblical praise - the song book of the Church, provided and inspired for that purpose. They were of course rich in their contemporary significance to Israel, as songs of inspiration and hope. But they are in a real sense even richer in Christological significance for the New Testament Church, which is, indeed, why they are so often quoted. In a real sense they are timeless. They are songs designed to be sung by God's people in every age and it must he counted a tragedy that so many Christian Churches today fail to use these canonical and covenantal songs of Scripture in the worship of God.

Textual Evidence

By textual evidence is meant those texts or verses of Scripture which have a bearing on the issue of Biblical praise. In looking at this material we have to ascertain which words and passages are perceived to be relevant, and why.

It must surely be agreed that the Lord has provided in the book of Psalms a song book, at the very least for the Church of the Old Testament. It also must surely be agreed that the Psalms, in view of the place given to them in the New Testament continue to be appropriate materials for the worship of the Church of the New Covenant. But the question arises: Is there a command to sing songs of merely human composition? Is there divine authority to sing the hymns of Isaac Watts (1674-1748) or John Newton (1725-1807) or Charles Wesley (1757-1834) or Horatius Bonar (1808-1889), or other such hymn writers?

Advocates of non-canonical song will seek to find warrant for their songs somewhere in Scripture. A number of passages are appealed to in support of the use in congregational song of materials other than those found in Scripture itself. Passages claimed as hymn fragments in the New Testament are also cited by way of collateral support. We shall look at these passages of Scripture and our chief concern will be to ask whether they really do warrant the expansion of praise beyond the confines of the Bible's own praise book. It should perhaps be said in this connection that there are several words in the Greek New Testament, which in English translation can give rise to misunderstandings. For example, the word translated 'hymn' does not necessarily mean in the New Testament context what the word has come to mean in common English usage. The relevant Greek words found in the New Testament in relation to song are the nouns *psalmos, hymnos* and *ōdē*, and the verbs *hymneō* and *psallō*. We will examine the New Testament references in which these words or their derivatives appear.

Matthew 26: 30; Mark 14: 26

The disciples are gathered with Jesus for the Last Supper in the Upper Room. It is the Jewish Passover. We read that when they had sung a hymn (*hymnēsantes*) they went out to the Mount of Olives. What was this

"What was this 'hymn?' Commentators agree that this would have been one of the Hallel Psalms, from that group of Psalms from 113 to 118 commonly sung at the Passover"

'hymn?' Commentators agree that this would have been one of the Hallel Psalms, from that group of Psalms from 113 to 118 commonly sung at the Passover. *Hymnēsantes* is an aorist active participle, which here indicates simply an action in the past. In this case the meaning is, roughly, 'having hymned.' It is from the verb *hymneō*, which means simply 'to sing a hymn' or 'to sing praise.' Any of these Hallel Psalms would have been appropriate to Jesus on the threshold of His crucifixion. It is as if Jesus takes these words as His own prayer in the gathering storm of His final days and hours on earth. He pledges to keep His vows in the presence of all the people (Psalm 116:12-19); He calls upon the Gentiles to join in God's praises (Psalm 117); and He concludes with a song of triumph: 'I shall not die, but live, and declare the works of the LORD' (Psalm 118:17). William Lane commented that, 'When Jesus arose to go to Gethsemane, Psalm 118 was upon his lips. It provided an appropriate description of how God would guide his

Messiah through distress and suffering to glory.' So here, at least, this reference to 'hymn,' rather than pointing to any uninspired song of praise, points to the Psalter.

Acts 16: 25; Hebrews 2:12

Paul and Silas have taken the gospel to Europe. There is encouragement (Acts 16:11-15). But there is also opposition. They are imprisoned in Philippi (vv.16-24). Are they downcast? Not a bit of it! After all, Jesus had encouraged rejoicing in just such situations (Matthew 5:12). At midnight, with their feet in the stocks in an inner prison, Paul and Silas are heard 'praying and singing hymns (*hymnoun*) to God' (v.25). This word *hymnoun* is an imperfect of the verb, *hymneō*; indicating continuing action. What were they singing? We do not know for sure, of course. But the suggestion of Addison Alexander commends itself: '*Praying, hymned* (or *sang to*) God, seems to express, not two distinct acts ... but the single act of lyrical worship, or praying ... by singing or chanting, perhaps one or more of the passages in the Book of Psalms peculiarly adapted and intended for the use of prisoners and others under persecution.'

Clearly whatever Paul and Silas sang that night was something they knew by heart. 'The explanation doubtless is,' says Professor William Binnie, 'that they had been taught to say and sing the Psalms in their childhood; and that their habitual attendance in the Synagogue and participation in its services had prevented the early familiarity with 'the praises of Israel' from being lost or impaired.'

This understanding of *hymnoun* here is strengthened by the reference in Hebrews 2:12 - the only other place in the New Testament where this verb is found. This is in fact found in a quotation from a Psalm! Speaking of Jesus' brotherly relations with believers the writer quotes Psalm 22:22: 'I will declare your name to my brethren; In the midst of the congregation I will sing praise [*hymnesō*] to you.'

1 Corinthians 14:26

The word *Psalmos* is found in 1 Corinthians 14: 'How is it then, brethren? Whenever you come together, each of you has a psalm (*psalmon*)...' (verse 26). C. K. Barrett suggests that this may be 'a fresh, perhaps spontaneous, composition, not an Old Testament psalm.' However, it would most likely be 'charismatic' - the question of the 'charismata' is the issue in that chapter. Besides this, Paul is speaking of the utterances of *individuals*. It is not likely that these would be *congregational* songs and in any case they would be directly Spirit-inspired. In addition, as Ralph Martin has observed, 'nothing ... is known of the content or form of such spontaneous creations' - assuming, that is, that they were not Bible Psalms, which in fact they may well have been. In other words, it would be unsafe to read too much into this reference.

Ephesians 5:19; Colossians 3:16

We come now to the two passages most commonly used in support of a warrant for the adoption of uninspired hymnody. 'Look,' someone will say, 'surely these verses indicate that we can use more than the Old Testament Psalms!' The nouns, *psalmos*, *hymnos* and *ōdē* are found together in both these passages. In an article written some years ago, Robert Morey claimed that 'the mention of "hymns" and "songs" clearly reveals that we can sing other materials than the Psalms.' This is a common view. But does it give any such warrant? Is it sustainable? Let us see.

In these verses Paul is certainly concerned with worship. He is also speaking of the believer's inward life. He exhorts the Ephesian Christians to be 'filled with the Spirit' (5:18). To the Colossian believers he says: 'let the word of Christ dwell in you richly in all wisdom' (3:16). The infilling of the Spirit, of course, brings the word of Christ to the heart, for it is the Holy Spirit's task to 'take the things of Christ' and declare them to the disciples (John 16:15). Paul puts this so tellingly to the Romans: 'if the Spirit of him who raised Jesus from the dead dwells in you, he who

> "Would compositions of men, not immediately inspired by the Spirit of God, qualify as the 'word of Christ' with which the believers were to be filled?"

raised Christ from the dead will also give life to your mortal bodies through his Spirit who dwells in you' (Romans 8:11). A consequence of the indwelling Spirit is praise. So, Paul enjoins the Ephesian and Colossian Christians to 'speak' or 'teach and admonish' each other through the medium of 'psalms, and hymns and spiritual songs', singing and making melody to the Lord with grace in their hearts (Ephesians 5:19; Colossians 3:16).

The question is: what exactly are these 'psalms, hymns and spiritual songs'? It goes without saying that every Christian will be happy to sing the songs to which Paul is referring here. It must of course be assumed that these were existing compositions, otherwise his Ephesian and Colossian readers would simply he bemused by the reference. But to what compositions would he be referring? To the end of his ministry Paul had a high view of Scripture (cf. 2 Timothy 3:14-17). Would compositions of men, not immediately inspired by the Spirit of God, qualify as the 'word of Christ' with which the believers were to be filled? It surely stretches credulity to maintain that they were non-inspired materials or that the Apostle was giving a free hand to post-apostolic writers to go ahead and compose their own hymns for use in worship.

To be sure, we cannot be certain about how Paul's hearers would have understood him. Commentators are by and large agreed that there is no general agreement about the meaning of this threefold description! Nor is there general agreement as to whether the adjective *pneumatikais* ('spiritual') qualifies only *ōdē* ('song'), or all three terms. F. F. Bruce's comment is representative: 'It is unlikely that any sharply demarcated division is intended, although the "psalms" might be drawn from the OT Psalter (which has supplied the chief vehicle for Christian praise from primitive times), the "hymns" might be Christian canticles, and the "spiritual songs" might be unpremeditated words sung "in the Spirit," voicing holy aspirations.' We cannot fail to notice how this paragraph of Bruce's is so replete with 'mights.' and vague suggestions. There is no positive evidence in these verses to warrant the conclusion that Paul was referring to three distinct groups or types of compositions, although no doubt the words had their distinctive meanings indicating the variety and richness of the songs Paul has in mind. There is simply no warrant for taking Ephesians 5:19 and Colossians 3:16 as justification for the adoption of uninspired hymnody in the worship of God. That would have these verses support far more than sound exegesis can sustain.

It seems perfectly reasonable, however, to take the references to psalms, hymns and spiritual songs as referring collectively to the Psalter. The various Greek words would be familiar to the New Testament Church as being found in the Old Testament Greek translation (the Septuagint or LXX) which was commonly in use. In the Septuagint the Psalm titles frequently contained these terms. In many cases more than one of the terms is used in a title, and in at least one instance all three terms are found in the title (Psalm 76)!

♦ *Psalmos* occurs 87 times in the Greek Old Testament, 67 times in the Psalm titles. In the New Testament this word occurs seven times: in each of the verses presently being considered, four times with reference to the book of Psalms (Luke 20:42, 24:44 and Acts 1:20, 13:33) and once in 1 Corinthians 14:26, where the reference is either to the Biblical Psalms or perhaps to a charismatic utterance, in which case the song would be individual and Spirit-inspired.

♦ *Hymnos* occurs 17 times, 13 times in the Psalms, six of which are in the titles. In the New Testament this word only occurs in the verses under examination.

♦ *Ōdē* occurs 80 times, 36 in Psalm titles and many other times within the Psalms themselves.

As we have seen, the word *hymneō* is used of the Book of Psalms (cf. Hebrews 2:12). *Ōdē* can also be used of the Psalms, although in the New Testament, apart from the texts in Ephesians and Colossians, the word is only found in the Book of Revelation (5:9; 14:3; 15:3), where the 'new song' refers neither to modern hymns nor any uninspired compositions. In connection with the passages in Ephesians and Colossians, Schlier comments: 'It is "spiritual", i.e., has a measure of inspiration (Eph. 5:19). Hence it is not an expression of personal feeling or experience but a "word of Christ" (Col. 3:16).'

There is strength, therefore, in the interpretation that understands Paul as using these three terms, *psalmos*, *hymnos* and *ōdē*, with reference to the Book of Psalms. These would correspond broadly to the Hebrew terms *mizmorim*, *tehillim* and *shirim* - the types of composition found in the Old Testament Psalter. As Thomas Manton (1620-1677) wrote: 'In Col.iii.16, and Eph. v. 19, Paul biddeth us "speak to one another in psalms and hymns and spiritual songs." Now these words (which are the known division of David's psalms, and expressly answering to the Hebrew words *Shurim*, *Tehillim*, and *Mizmorim*, by which his psalms are distinguished and entitled), being so precisely used by the apostle in both places, do plainly point us to the Book of Psalms.' No doubt the terms do reflect different types of Psalms and Paul would be implying, what we know to be the case, that there are Psalms which relate to the whole range of our spiritual needs. It is interesting that in other places in the Old and New Testaments threefold descriptions of similar things are given. For example, in Exodus 34:7 we find 'iniquity and transgression and sin.' In Deuteronomy 5:31 and 6:1 we find 'commandments and statutes and judgments.' In Acts 2:22 we find the phrase, 'miracles, wonders, and signs.'

This understanding of Ephesians 5:19 and Colossians 3:16 was a common understanding amongst the Puritans. This is clear from a Preface to a 1673 edition of the Scottish Metrical Psalter of 1650, subscribed, among others, by Thomas Manton, John Owen, Thomas Watson, Matthew Poole, Thomas Vincent, and Edward Calamy. In the Preface it is stated that 'though spiritual songs of mere human composure may have their use, yet our devotion is best secured, where the matter and words are of immediately divine inspiration; and to us David's Psalms seem plainly intended by those terms of "psalms and hymns and spiritual songs," which the apostle useth (Eph. 5:19; Col. 3:16).' This general perspective also finds broad support in some older commentators like Jean Daillé (1594-1670) and William Binnie (1823-1886), and in more recent years has been ably expounded by Professor John Murray and William Young in a *Report* they produced for the Orthodox Presbyterian Church in 1947.

Someone might still object that this interpretation is a little speculative and less than conclusive. But Paul is clearly saying *something*, and the case seems to be much stronger for the view which sees exclusive reference to the Psalter in these verses. At any rate, it can be seen that these texts do not provide any positive warrant for the adoption of non-inspired extra-scriptural materials of praise as congregational song. Neither these texts, not any other related New Testament passages, provide any support for the introduction of uninspired human hymns into Christian public worship. Furthermore, let it be said that no Christian is *bound* to sing any songs which the Lord, in His wisdom, has not *commanded* them to sing or *provided* for their singing, however good such songs may appear to be on a human level.

James 5:13; Romans 15:9

The last word we shall look at is the verb *psallō*, 'to sing psalms, or praises.' James encourages those who are suffering to pray. He encourages those who are cheerful to 'sing psalms' (*psalletō*). What has James in mind here? Well, this word, *psallō*, appears 56 times in the Septuagint, predominantly in the Psalms. It came to mean, generally, a song of praise. Now, of course this cannot be shown conclusively to refer to Biblical Psalms. However, as the Puritan writer, Thomas Manton, suggests: 'In the original there is but one word, *psalletō*, let him sing; but because the apostle is pressing them to religious use of every condition, and because this is the usual acception of the word *psalletō* in the church, it is well rendered "let him sing psalms".

The use of *psallō* in another New Testament context indicates that Manton's interpretation is a sound one. In Romans 15:9, the only other place in the New Testament where this word appears, Paul finds Biblical support for the Gentiles to praise God. Where? Well, in the Psalms of course! Jesus Christ came, says Paul, 'that the Gentiles might glorify God for his mercy, as it is written: "For this reason I will confess to you among the Gentiles, and sing [*psalō*] to your name" (Psalm 18:49).' There is simply no advocacy of the use of uninspired songs of praise in public worship in any of the references which either refer to worship itself, or use the language relevant to the content of biblical praise.

New Testament 'Christian Hymns'

There are some songs in the New Testament. In Luke's gospel, for instance, there are the songs of Mary (1:46-55), Zacharias (1:68-79) and Simeon (2:29-32). These are certainly Spirit-inspired songs, and whilst there does not seem to be any objection in principle to their use in public worship, it is not altogether clear that even these songs were intended by the Lord for such a purpose.

There are, however, other passages which some have suggested are fragments of hymn-type compositions. These 'fragments', it is felt, bear witness to a developing liturgical tradition in the early Church. Ephesians 5:14; Philippians 2:6-11; Colossians 1:15-20; and 1 Timothy 3:16 are appealed to as illustrating this point. What are we to make of such claims?

1. *The procedure is speculative.* However confident the claims may be that there are hymn-citations in the New

Testament, there is no uncontradicted proof that this is the case. Binnie rightly called such claims 'precarious.' Much ingenious and careful research has been done. Despite this there is still a lack of universal agreement amongst scholars on the precise nature of these verses. It cannot be shown that they were ever sung and it would seem that no two New Testament writers quote from the same 'hymn' fragment and

> "If the Holy Spirit had meant the Church to use them, it is inconceivable that He would simply have left fragments here and there, and not ensured that the compositions (if they were such) were preserved in their entirety"

no one writer quotes from the same 'hymn' fragment twice! Commenting on the subject, the 'songs of Primitive Christianity', Delling makes the significant observation that, 'Attempts have been made to distinguish Christian hymns in the New Testament, but these are hypothetical in the absence of discernible laws.' He also makes the obvious point that '...the mere presence of lofty speech or integrated structure does not have to denote a hymn.'

2. *The procedure is inconclusive.* Even supposing that it could be proved conclusively that hymn fragments were to be found in the New Testament, that would still not prove that these items were part of a developing liturgical tradition. For one thing, the providence of God is against it. In this way: none of the items of which the various verses in the New Testament are taken to be fragments has come down to us. The writers might indeed have gleaned these 'fragments' from contemporary songs, but why then did these songs not come down in their entirety if they were to

be used by the Church, or if they were to be part of a liturgical tradition? What sort of tradition is it that fails to retain such items? If the Holy Spirit had meant the Church to use them, it is inconceivable that He would simply have left fragments here and there, and not ensured that the compositions (if they were such) were preserved in their entirety.

There is no evidence that these passages were either songs or part of a developing liturgical tradition. But even supposing the passages were found to be songs or parts of songs, it does not follow that this provides some sort of warrant for the use of uninspired hymns in worship or demonstrable proof that they were ever used in worship services. This whole area of New Testament studies is marvellously imaginative, but entirely inconclusive as far the question of New Testament praise is concerned.

IV. THE REGULATIVE PRINCIPLE

All Christian Churches are regulated in one way or another. It might be expected that all Churches would at least claim to be regulated by the Scriptures. In many instances, however, Churches have deviated from the Scriptures as their rule of doctrine and practice. In the history of the Church this has become a particular focus of discussion and differences. What requires to be examined is how Churches have developed and applied a 'regulative principle', particularly on the question of worship.

What regulates Church life?

Most Churches would hold to some sort of Biblical authority behind their government and practice. However, under various social and secularist pressures the application of Biblical authority in Church life has diminished or been modified in most 'main-line' Churches. The higher critical movement, which arose in the mid-nineteenth century, produced considerable pressure for a change in the Church's view of Biblical authority, a pressure continued through the twentieth century into the twenty-first century both in Old Testament and New Testament critical approaches. Gradually the Bible was reckoned not to be sufficient to provide an exclusive source for doctrine and government in the Church. If a Church does not accept the full inspiration and sufficiency of the Bible as God's Word, this will have a profound effect on how it will regulate its affairs. The regulative principle thus adopted will be influenced by man-centred considerations and perhaps even by largely social or political concerns.

Is this a matter of indifference?
At the same time there are some who do accept the inspiration and authority of the Bible in an orthodox sense and yet do not consider that the Bible provides sufficient materials for the regulation of worship and government in the Church. Many churchmen of a conservative evangelical standpoint maintain that the Church is largely to be left to its own discretion in these areas of Church practice. They may even point to a section of the *Westminster Confession of Faith* for support: 'there are some circumstances concerning the worship of God, and government of the Church, common to human actions and societies, which are to be ordered by the light of nature, and Christian prudence, according to the general rules of the Word, which are always to be observed' (I:6). What is referred to there, however, are circumstances *common to human actions and societies*. The worship of God, and most specifically its content, the form of Church Government, and the offices and sacraments of the Church, are, however, the *distinctives* of the Church and scarcely 'common to human actions and societies'! The *Confession* at that point simply refers to some outward circumstances, such as times and places of services, Church records and buildings, Church finances and the like. So the question of a Church's stated, or implicit, regulative principle is of far-reaching significance, not least in the matter of determining the content of praise, an area in which denominational peculiarities, distinctives or prejudices will find expression.

> "Worship was not to be set up according to man's desires, but according to the express commandments of God"

What 'regulative principle' is found in Scripture?

The question, therefore, needs to be asked: What is the Church's regulative principle? Is it sound? Is it Biblical? What are the practical implications of this for the Church's government and worship? The Churches of the Old and New Testaments were to be regulated in their government and worship, as well as in their doctrine. They were regulated by God's express will. To go beyond the revealed will of God was found to be perilous, as Nadab and Abihu found (Leviticus 10:1-3); as King Saul found (1 Samuel 13:13-14); as King Solomon found (1 Kings 11:9-11); as Israel found (Ezekiel 5:5-8; Malachi 2:1-17); as the Pharisees in Jesus' day found (Mark 7:6-13); as Dives found (Luke 16:19-31, especially vv. 29-31); and as so many of the Churches spoken of in the Book of Revelation found (Chapters 2 and 3).

The particular law in focus, expressive of the word and will of God, was the Decalogue - the Ten Commandments. The common factor was the violation of the will of God in connection with His worship. It was violation, essentially, of the second commandment (Exodus 20:4-6). Worship was not to be set up according to man's desires, but according to the express commandments of God. That this is not a strange principle in the New Testament context is sufficiently shown in a passage such as Matthew chapter 15, verse 9, in which Jesus draws on the prophet Isaiah in castigating the hypocrites who subverted the commandments of God, expressed in the Decalogue, through their additions. Paul, similarly, in his letter to the Colossians, contrasts the commandments of God and the commandments of men in relation to the devotional life (cf. Colossians 2:20-23). The word and will of God, then, are to be paramount! That is the consistent message of Old and New Testaments. In the older covenant the principle was 'keep my commandments' (Exodus 20:4-6). 'Whatever I command you, be careful to observe it; you shall not add to it nor take away from it' (Deuteronomy 12:32). There were blessings attaching to obedience: as Moses found (Deuteronomy 4:1-2, 39-40); as Noah found (Genesis 6:22; 7:5-7; cf. Hebrews 11:7); as the Children of Israel found (Jeremiah 7:23-24). The last chapter of the book of Exodus is a model of the Old Testament regulative principle.

In the New Testament, too, we find a similar attitude. In His teaching on prayer the Lord Jesus Christ includes the petition 'Your will be done, on earth as it is in heaven' (Matthew 6:10; Luke 11:2). Furthermore, Jesus gives commission to His disciples to go into the world with the gospel message. He spells out their task: 'teaching them to observe *all things I have commanded you*' (Matthew 28:20). He says, 'if you love me, keep my commandments' (John 14:15; cf. John 15:14; 1 John 5:3).

In other words, the regulative principle of the New Testament Church is consistent with that of the Old Testament. The New Testament Church is to comply with the Saviour's stated wishes. To help in this, of course, the Holy Spirit was sent to the Church, to represent Christ, to extend the Kingdom (John 3:3,5), to ensure the completion of the Scriptures, and to enable subsequent generations to understand and comply with them (cf. John 14:26; 16:7-8; Acts 2:33). It is significant that at the close of the canon of Holy Scripture there is a warning, a regulative principle (Revelation 22:18-19; cf. Deuteronomy 4:2). The New Testament contains clear principles and regulations governing the life of the Christian Church. There are principles and regulations, for example, in connection with office bearers (Acts 6:1-7; 1 Timothy 3:1-13 [cf.

4:11 and 5:21]; Titus 1:5-9 &c.); in connection with the Lord's Supper (Matthew 26:26-30; 1 Corinthians 11:23); in connection with Paul's teaching (cf. 1 Corinthians 2:12-16; Galatians 1:12). The over-riding concern is to know and do the will of the Lord.

How does this principle apply today?

The responsibility of the Christian Church today, no less than in the first century of the Christian era, is to conform to the revealed will of God. It is intended that the Church be based upon 'the foundation of the apostles and prophets, Jesus Christ himself being the chief cornerstone' (Ephesians 2:20). Therefore the will of Christ is paramount.

It is true that the Bible requires to be properly interpreted and that differences can arise in that connection. It is necessary that the principles of the Scriptures be grasped as clearly as possible, with sincerity and a good conscience (Romans 14:5). A Church's regulative principle in Christian faith and life by and large will be determined by a combination of the following factors: (a) the perceived *authority* of the Bible; (b) the acceptance of the *sufficiency* of Scripture; and (c) the application of a sound Biblical *method of interpretation*.

What regulative principle should apply in the Church?

A Church or body of professing Christians with a weak view of the authority of the Bible and its sufficiency, or a liberal and critical approach to Scripture, will have a very different pattern of doctrine and worship from a Church or body of professing Christians which has a high view of Scripture and its sufficiency. What interests us here is how such views have affected the development of praise materials adopted within Churches. Two main views have arisen, at least within evangelical Protestantism.

1. *The Lutheran or Anglican view.* The view of the regulative principle associated with the Lutheran or Anglican outlook is one which basically maintains that anything may be admitted to the worship or practice of the Church provided it is not *forbidden* or

proscribed by the Word of God. In one form or another this is the predominant view in the Church today. This broader or looser view is expressed, for example, in Article XX of the *39 Articles of the Church of England* (1571) which states that: 'The Church hath power to decree Rites or Ceremonies, and authority in Controversies of Faith: And yet it is not lawful for the Church to ordain any thing that is contrary to God's word written.' In other words, anything may be admitted provided it is not prohibited. It will be recognized how far-reaching this principle might be. For example, as Professor Petticrew put it in 1902, accepting this idea would allow such things as, 'the sign of the cross in Baptism ... bowing to the East, the wearing of symbolical vestments, the lighting of wax candles in churches in the daytime, the ceremonial use of incense, holy water ... the elevation of the host, &c, &c, for *none* of these things is *expressly forbidden* in Scripture.'

One can see how this broad principle could be the occasion, not only of the addition of all sorts of things not commanded in the Bible, but also of a serious imposition on people's consciences. No one can be bound by anything which is not entirely Biblical. This do-what-is-not-forbidden approach really states that what the Church says, either as a denomination, or for that matter as a local congregation, goes. It is hard to see how this does not amount to the imposition of commandments of men (cf. Matthew 15:6, 9; Mark 7:6-13; Colossians 2:18-23).

2. *The Reformed or Calvinistic view.* This view states that only what is *prescribed* in the word of God is warranted. This was the approach of the Reformed Churches. It maintains that the Church is bound by what God has been pleased to reveal in the Holy Scriptures. Needless to say this implies a high view of Scripture and its sufficiency and application in all matters of faith and worship. *The Westminster Confession of Faith* (1647) expresses this well, when it declares that, 'it pleased the Lord, at sundry times, and in divers manners, to reveal Himself, and to declare that His will unto His Church; and afterwards, for the better preserving and propagating of the truth, and for the more sure establishment

and comfort of the Church against the corruption of the flesh, and the malice of Satan and of the world, to commit the same wholly unto writing: which maketh the Holy Scripture to be most necessary; those former ways of God's revealing His will unto His people being now ceased' (I:1).

The implication of this, as it applied to worship, was seen to be that, 'the acceptable way of worshipping the true God is instituted by Himself, and so limited by His own revealed will, that He may not be worshipped according to the imaginations and devices of men, or the suggestions of Satan, under any visible representation, or any other way not prescribed in the holy Scripture' (XXI:1). This is in perfect agreement with the regulative principle evident in the Scriptures themselves and outlined above.

The principle is well stated by the outstanding Scottish Reformed theologian, William Cunningham (1805-1861): 'The Calvinistic section of the Reformers ... were of the opinion that there are sufficiently plain indications in Scripture itself, that it was Christ's mind and will, that nothing should be introduced into the government and worship of the church, unless a positive warrant for it could be found in Scripture. This principle was adopted and acted upon by the English Puritans and the Scottish Presbyterians; and we are persuaded that it is the only true and safe principle applicable to this matter.' As far as the implications of this principle are concerned, Cunningham goes on to point out that, 'if it were fully carried out, [it] would just be to leave the church in the condition in which it was left by the apostles, in so far as we have any means of information; a result, surely, which need not be very alarming, except to those who think that they themselves have very superior powers for improving and adorning the church by their inventions.'

What about freedoms allowed in the New Testament?
There are two points raised by advocates of non-canonical praise materials which are felt to qualify the more rigorous application of the regulative principle.

1. *The analogy with prayer and preaching.* It is maintained by some that as there is freedom allowed in the New Testament in preaching and in prayer, by analogy freedom ought to be allowed also in the use of suitable songs of human composition. Each element, however, must have its own warrant from the Word of God. The requirements for these different elements of worship services are not identical. What distinguishes the singing of praise from prayer and preaching is this: (a) there is clear precedent (and therefore warrant) for 'free' prayer and preaching; and, (b) as in its nature the singing of praise is something that engages *all* the worshippers it therefore must involve a form (canon?) of material which *all* can engage in without any violation of conscience. Whatever the merits of non-inspired materials, they are after all not immediately inspired by the Lord. One can never say, 'these were given by the Lord for the use of all Christian worshippers'. The fact is that God has given a manual or Book of Praises in the Psalms. Is it not presumptuous to impose some other 'canon' of sung praise which in the final analysis is not God's Word? In their nature prayer and preaching are 'free'. The praise, however, is akin to the reading of Scripture. In its nature

> "The fact is that God has given a manual or Book of Praises in the Psalms. Is it not presumptuous to impose some other 'canon' of sung praise which in the final analysis is not God's Word?"

Songs of the Spirit

it must be a fixed manual. Just as we would not expect Scripture reading in Public Worship to be supplanted by readings from the works of mere men, by the same token we should not expect the congregational songs to be other than God-given songs.

2. *The demands of the expansion of revelation.* Some will say that the expansion of revelation in the New Testament justifies the extension of praise beyond what we have in the Old Testament. However, as John Murray points out that, 'We have no evidence either from the Old Testament or from the New that the expansion of revelation received expression in the devotional exercises of the church through the singing of uninspired songs of praise. This is a fact that cannot be discounted.'

It is suggested that some hymns can express truth better than the psalms, especially in relation to the themes of the gospel. This implies that somehow man has to make up what God has left out, namely, produce song based on New Testament material. But who decides which of such materials are, and which are not, to be used by the whole Church? This is not only potentially destructive of uniformity of worship, but also of unity in worship.

The giving of the Spirit at Pentecost did of course make a profound difference in the Church. But it is presumptuous to imply from this that there is thus a competence given to the Church to add non-canonical materials for congregational song. There was new revelation, of course, inscripturated in the New Testament, though, significantly, no separate manual of praise. In his outstanding work on the Holy Spirit George Smeaton was to say this about the psalms in relation to their relevance for the Christian Church: 'No book of a similar kind was prepared for the New Testament Church. The Holy Spirit, replenishing the sweet singers of Israel with spiritual truth and holy love, anticipated in this way much of the necessity that should be felt in Christian times...They describe the eternity and omnipresence, the majesty and condescension, the justice and mercy of God in a strain of the most fervid devotion. They sing of repentance and faith, of joy in God and delight in God's law, with an ardour beyond which it is impossible to go. They depict Christ's royal reign and His union with His Church; the anointing with the oil of gladness (Ps. xlv. 7); the receiving of gifts for men (Pa. lxviii. 18); and the supreme dominion with which Christ was to be invested by the Father with a tenderness, unction, and joy, to which no other words are equal. And those psalms which are called "new songs" anticipate the full millennial glory.'

It is interesting that in the post-resurrection appearance of Christ to the disciples on the road to Emmaus (Luke 24:13-35) Jesus at one point rebukes them as 'foolish ones, and slow in heart to believe all that the prophets have spoken! Ought not Christ to have suffered these things and to enter into his glory?' (vv.25-26). To this is added: 'And beginning at Moses and all the prophets, he expounded to them in all the Scriptures the things concerning himself' (v.27). The New Testament is, of course, very necessary. The Spirit's coming did shed light on the meaning of the Old Testament. But this does not mean we have to resort to uninspired materials of praise in congregational song. The Spirit will most certainly enable the people of God not to be 'slow in heart' to understand Christ in all the Psalms! Properly understood the Psalms do, we maintain, constitute a sufficient volume for praise for the Christian Church. The Psalms were given by Christ, and may all be understood to speak of Him and His works.

It is maintained, therefore, that Churches holding to the authority and sufficiency of the Bible as God's Word written, should apply the principle that 'what Scripture does not prescribe, it forbids.' This in turn will encourage the Church to look for warrant and provision in the matter of the content of its praises, and to be circumspect concerning anything that derived from mere human invention or taste. If the Church confined itself to what derives from Scripture precept or example it would have a perfectly adequate directory for worship and government. That is the sphere of its discretion. It is the consistent application of this principle which is the basis of our appeal for the use as song in public worship only of the songs of praise found in Holy Scripture.

V. THE HISTORICAL TESTIMONY

Early Church

Evidence for exclusive psalm singing in the immediately post-Apostolic Church is strong. One historian has concluded that, 'those who contend for the exclusive use of the Scripture Psalter, in the direct and formal praise of God, find in the history of the early Church signal confirmation of their position.' A more recent hymnologist agrees, 'In the Western Church, the hymn was slower in winning its way

"Philip Schaff reminds us: 'We have no complete religious song remaining from the period of persecution (i.e. the first three centuries) except the song of Clement of Alexandria to the divine Logos - which, however, cannot be called a hymn.'"

largely because of the prejudice against non-Scriptural praise, and not until nearly the end of the fourth century was hymn-singing beginning to be practised in the churches.' This is confirmed by the fact that the 59th clause of the Council of Laodicea (314-372) decreed this: "Forbids to sing uninspired hymns &c., in church, and to read the uncanonical books."

To some degree this attitude in the early church arose out of a concern to establish the New Testament canon. The churches were aware of the distinctiveness of canonical literature. Cecil Northcott, in the quotation just given, is unfair to use the term 'prejudice' as he does. After all, he might just as easily have commended the early church for the concern evident for exclusively Biblical praise. The real prejudice seems to be on Northcott's part.

There is confirmation of this early church practice from the negative side. It is clear that Psalm-singing was widespread. But as Philip Schaff reminds us: 'We have no complete religious song remaining from the period of persecution (i.e. the first three centuries) except the song of Clement of Alexandria to the divine Logos - which, however, cannot be called a hymn.'

While there is abundant evidence of the use of Bible Psalms in the worship of the early post-Apostolic Church, there is an absence of evidence for the use of anything but the Psalms in the direct and formal praise of the Churches.

Reformation Church
The Reformation movement was not a unified one. There were different strands within what is broadly called the Reformation of the sixteenth century. Martin Luther (1483-1546) and John Calvin (1509-1564) were both concerned for reformation in the Church, but they differed in their convictions on the regulative principle, as indicated above. However, the supporters of the Calvinistic Reformation movement emphasized that specific warrant or 'express commandment,' as the Scottish Reformer John Knox put it, was necessary for every aspect of the divine service. John Calvin expressed it this way: 'all the parts of divine worship ... the Lord has faithfully comprehended, and clearly unfolded, in his sacred oracles.'

The 1563 *Heidelberg Catechism* asks the question, 'What doth God require in the second commandment?' and answers by saying, 'That we in no wise represent God by images, nor worship him in any other way than he has commanded in his word.'

The Reformation period saw a revival of congregational singing and specifically of the singing of Biblical Psalms. The Psalms were, by and large, the 'Hymn Book' of the Reformation Churches. As Millar Patrick observed, 'at a stroke the Reformed

Church cut itself loose from the entire mass of Latin hymns and from the use of hymnody in general, and adopted the Psalms of the Old Testament as the sole medium of Church praise.'

It is true that some of the Reformers, such as John Calvin, attached the Canticles, the Ten Commandments in metre, the Lord's Prayer, and the Apostles' Creed, to their Psalters. This, however, is scarcely an advocacy of uninspired hymnody. Calvin himself maintained that, 'We cannot find better songs than David's Psalms: which the Holy Spirit has spoken and created.'

It should be understood that for the Reformers the use of Bible Psalms was a very positive thing. This is scarcely better stated than by Calvin in the 'Introduction' to his Commentary on the Psalms: 'There is no other book in which there is to be found more express and magnificent commendations, both of the unparalleled liberality of God towards his Church, and of all his works; there is no other book in which there is recorded so many deliverances, nor one in which the evidences and experiences of the fatherly providence and solicitude which God exercises towards us, are celebrated with such splendour of diction, and yet with the strictest adherence to truth; in short, there is no other book in which we are more perfectly taught the right manner of praising God, or in which we are more powerfully stirred up to the performance of this religious exercise.'

It is clear that the Reformers' adoption of the Psalms arose both from a profound respect for their nature as compositions immediately inspired by the Holy Spirit, and from a positive awareness of their inherent beauty and truth in spiritual terms. It did not seem to be any disadvantage in the development of their Christian piety that they used only these materials in praise drawn exclusively from God's inspired book.

Puritans

The attitude and approach of the seventeenth-century English Puritans is well expressed in the *Westminster Confession of Faith* (1647), arguably the high water mark of the Confessions of the Reformed Churches in the English-speaking world. The *Confession*, besides being clear on the regulative principle governing worship and practice within the Church, also specifically enjoins 'the singing of psalms with grace in the heart.' If any proof of the Westminster Assembly's concern for Psalm singing is needed, then surely it is well established by the fact that it sponsored a metrical translation of the 150 Psalms of Scripture. This was the basis of the *Scottish Psalter* of 1650. There is no doubt that the Puritan Churches were Psalm-singing Churches. In a Puritan Preface to a 1673 edition of the Scottish Psalter of 1650, referred to above, it was noted that, in their opinion, 'The translation which is now put into thy hands cometh nearest to the original of any that we have seen, and runneth with such fluent sweetness, that we thought fit to recommend it to thy Christian acceptance...' In other words, that Psalter was not seen to be a mere paraphrase of the Psalms. D. H. Hislop was surely correct when he observed that, 'The exclusive use of the Psalter is derived from its [i.e., the Reformed or Calvinistic] conception of revelation.'

The Puritans basically operated from the same principles as the Reformation Churches. That prince of Puritan theologians, John Owen (1616-1683), for example, spoke with no uncertain sound: 'A principal part of the duty of the church in this matter [i.e., of worship] is, to take care that nothing be admitted or practised in the worship of God, or as belonging thereunto, which is not instituted and appointed by the Lord Christ. In its care, faithfulness, and watchfulness herein consists the principal part of its loyalty unto the Lord Jesus, as the head, king, and lawgiver of his church; and which to stir us up unto, he hath left so many severe interdictions and prohibitions in his word, against all *additions* to his commands, upon any pretence whatever.'

Owen was unhappy about the persuasion of some that the Lord had not prescribed every element of His worship and describes this as a case of 'negligence in enquiring after what he hath so prescribed.' The following century saw the beginnings of the introduction of non-inspired materials for praise into the worship services of the Churches. This was promoted most notably by the Independent, Isaac Watts (1674-1748), perhaps the founding father of English hymnody, and, later, the *Olney hymns* (1779) of John Newton (1725-1807) and William Cowper (1731-1800). Watts produced what he considered 'Christianized' versions of the Psalms. He presumably felt that the Lord had overlooked doing this in the New Testament era. But these were men of their times. It was the time, supposedly, of 'Enlightenment.' As a result of the intellectual and philosophical movements of this time, the Churches came under pressure to modify previously held positions on the nature and sufficiency of divine revelation. Human reason was seen to be perfectly adequate in connection with the affairs of this world. People apparently no longer needed to be constrained by the earlier ideas of Scriptural authority.

In the matter of the content of praise in the Church, one can see how there would be pressure to extend the praise items used by the addition of materials of merely human composition, however much it implied omissions by the Lord from what became the canon of New Testament. Amongst those who raised their voices against this tendency was William Romaine (1714-1795), an Anglican minister who wrote in 1775 that, 'our hymn-mongers ... shut out the Psalms, to introduce their own verses into the Church, sing them with great delight, and, as they fancy, with great profit, although the practice be in direct opposition to the command of God, and, therefore, cannot possibly be accompanied with the divine blessing.'

The situation has advanced apace since then. Today it seems that there is, as Owen put it in his day, 'negligence in enquiring' after what God has prescribed (or, for that matter, proscribed) in the matter of worship. There is today a continuous flow of hymns and verses produced for Christian worship, largely satisfying the demands of passing trends, and many Churches seem to be more and more detached from praise and practice drawn from the Scriptures. Are we to look back with pity that these Puritans 'only' praised the Lord with the Psalms and did not have the benefit of the hymnody of later years; or will we not rather have to lament the fact that the Church today in general does not have such a firm grasp of the glorious truths and experiential realities of the Word of God that the earlier generations enjoyed?

Presbyterians

The Presbyterian Churches in Scotland from the time of the Reformation through the seventeenth-century Covenanting period and up to the latter part of the

"The Presbyterian Churches in Scotland from the time of the Reformation through the seventeenth-century Covenanting period and up to the latter part of the nineteenth-century were basically Psalm-singing Churches."

nineteenth-century were basically Psalm-singing Churches. The *Scottish Psalmody* produced in 1650 took a significant place and wielded an important influence in the life and culture of the nation throughout that period. The Psalter was the only authorized manual of praise, in that metrical form, right down to the late nineteenth century. In the previous century there had been a move to introduce in addition some *Scripture Paraphrases*, and many Psalters were produced with these *Paraphrases*, and five other 'Hymns,' bound in with the Psalms. This gave the impression of ecclesiastical sanction which did not actually exist. It is true that in 1781 the *Scottish Paraphrases* were given an interim approval for experimental use by the Church of Scotland. Legislation was never passed, however, subsequently giving explicit authorization for these songs.

It was not until 1861 that the Church of Scotland formally authorized hymns of merely human composition. The Free Church of Scotland followed suit in 1872, but not without controversy. James Macgregor (1830-1894), the Professor of Systematic Theology at New College Edinburgh, for one, was unhappy with this movement. He expressed his reservations in no uncertain terms in a 'Memorial' to the Free Church Assembly of 1869. Among other things, he was to say that, 'Our Church, for many generations, has not, in her congregational praise, made use of any materials of merely human inspiration, and that, with reference even to materials of divine inspiration, the ambiguous quasi-sanction attained by the "paraphrases" dates only from a very recent period of her history, and derives its origin from the deepest darkness of her "dark age" of moderatism.'

As to the five 'Hymns' often printed in the back of the Psalters, it was Macgregor's judgment that these were 'partly Socinian, mainly deistical, wholly unevangelical at heart,' and had been 'dragged in from the fly-leaf for the purpose of giving to the impression some colour of foundation in fact,' namely, that they had some ecclesiastical sanction, which in fact they did not possess. But this was a common approach of those who wished to introduce non-inspired materials for praise, thus cloaking a shift in attitude both as to the nature of revelation and the sufficiency of Scripture in matters of faith and practice. As late as 1884 the outstanding New Testament scholar Professor George Smeaton (1814-1889) resigned as an elder at the Grange Free Church, Edinburgh, over the introduction of the *Free Church Hymn Book* into that congregation.

Predictably there has been a gradual displacement of the Psalms from Presbyterian worship and along with this a growing discontent about the content of praise on the grounds that it apparently always needs to be contemporary. On reflection it may be observed that Jesus did not sing the hymns of the modern era;

the Apostles in the New Testament times did not sing the songs of
the modern era; and neither did the Reformers and Puritans. Were
they inferior Christians? Does that not demonstrate that it is not
necessary to sing hymns or songs of merely human composition
to have real, authentic, spiritual Christian worship? It is often said
that the Psalm-singing Churches are 'traditional.' In reality it is
the Hymn-singing Churches that are traditional, as they derive
their congregational song, in so far as they use non-canonical song,
entirely from human tradition!

This is not to say that the Church need be tied to a
metrical translation of a previous age, however much it may be
venerated. It is often argued against Metrical Psalms that they are
themselves paraphrases, after a fashion. A primary consideration
must be to have Psalms for singing which reflect accurately the
underlying Hebrew, with help from the Septuagint and New
Testament quotations in Greek. In 'Directions' prefixed to his
Calendar of Daily Readings first produced in 1842, Robert Murray
McCheyne (1813-1843) said this about the *Scottish Psalmody*:'It is
truly an admirable translation from the Hebrew, and is frequently
more correct than the prose version.' Improving translations is
no doubt always desirable, but at the same time it is important
that the translation is suited to congregational singing and easy to
understand. This was certainly the concern of the Reformers, and
those involved in the development of Psalmody arising from the
Westminster Assembly.

Revivals
It would probably be considered unimaginable today that there
could be genuine spiritual revival in a Church which uses only
Bible Psalms. The influence of the Psalms in the development and
spread of Christianity in the world may be well appreciated from all
that has already been outlined in this chapter. The fact is that the
Psalms have been significant at times of revival in Church history.
This should not be a surprise as the Psalms, in John Calvin's words,
are 'An Anatomy of all the Parts of the Soul.'

> "The piety of a people is in no small measure moulded by the praise they sing"

In a book entitled *The True Psalmody*, first produced in America in 1861, the observation is made that, 'The Waldenses sang the Psalms and nothing else in their Alpine valleys; ... The French Church, and the Churches of Switzerland, used nothing else in song, during the palmiest days of their religious life; while these sacred songs contributed not a little to the spread of the gospel. These Psalms constituted the only psalmody of the Scottish Church in her first and second Reformations ... These Psalms were the sacred songs of the revived church in Ireland.'

Of the effect of the metrical Psalter in connection with the eighteenth-century revivals in Scotland, Arthur Fawcett has suggested that, 'It is not possible to evaluate the tremendous significance of the metrical psalter; almost all the subjects of the revival - at least those whose stories we have - quoted from it. Again and again, it is from the remembered lines of its pages that light flashed into gloomy darkness.'

When one thinks that the piety of a people is in no small measure moulded by the praise they sing, the importance and significance of the Psalms becomes evident.

VI. CONCLUSIONS

No Christian can possibly deny that the worship of God is an extremely important matter. How are we to worship the Lord? Sings David, the 'sweet psalmist of Israel' (2 Samuel 23:1):

> Give unto the LORD,
> O you mighty ones,

> Give unto the LORD
>> glory and strength.
> Give unto the LORD
>> the glory due to His name;
> Worship the LORD
>> in the beauty of holiness.
>>> (Psalm 29:1-2).

The Old Testament Church asked the question: 'With what shall I come before the LORD, and bow myself before the High God? Shall I come before Him with burnt offerings, with calves a year old? Will the LORD be pleased with thousands of rams or ten thousand rivers of oil? Shall I give my first-born for my transgression, the fruit of my body for the sin of my soul?' What was the answer? 'He has shown you, O man, what is good...' (Micah 6:7-8). The Lord has shown us! Are we content with what the Lord has provided in His Word, or will we need to add something in order to make up what He has left incomplete?

It has been the burden of this book to suggest that in the matter of worship, the Lord has shown us what is good. He has provided materials in the Psalms sufficient for worship, and the introduction of merely human compositions, however nice their sentiments or spiritual their content, and however well-intentioned their advocates, is basically an act of human presumption. We believe the arguments in this connection are both sound and Scriptural. They are summarized here.

The Psalms are the fruit of divine inspiration

The Psalms are both intended and provided for singing in the Church. The fact is that only the Book of Psalms can be used with the certainty that these songs have been divinely appointed for the purpose. Even with the best of Hymn books there is not that assurance. The adoption of other, non-inspired materials of praise carries with it the implication that somehow something is missing from the Biblical provision in the matter of New Testament praise. William Romaine's words are challenging, as they are forthright:

'I want a name for a man who should pretend that he could make better hymns than the Holy Ghost ... why ... would any man in the world take it into his head to sit down and write hymns for the use of the Church? It is just the same as if he were to write a new Bible.'

The Psalms are sufficient for New Testament praise

Someone might say: 'Isn't the Book of Psalms unnecessarily restrictive? Surely we should use the name of Jesus in song?' This is a fair point. But Christ *is* in the Psalms. As O. Palmer Robertson, formerly Professor of Old Testament at Westminster Theological Seminary, has reminded us: 'In some ways, all the psalms refer to Christ, for each relates to the redemption he has accomplished for his people... All the psalms relate to Jesus Christ and his redeeming work.'

Besides this, think of the impact of the Psalms themselves in the New Testament. There are at least 150 Psalm citations in the New Testament. The argument of the Letter to the Hebrews is to a considerable degree tied in with the Psalms. Jesus Himself stated that the Psalms spoke of Him (Luke 24:44-47). They speak of His person, as a prophet (Psalm 2:7), as a priest (110:4; cf. Hebrews 5:6) and as a king (2:6; 45:6). They speak of His eternal sonship (2:7; cf. Hebrews 5:5), His advent (96:11-13) and His humanity (22, *passim*). They speak of His work (118:22; cf. Acts 4:11), in His sufferings and death (40:6-8; 21 *passim*; 22:1; 69:9; cf. Matthew 27:46), in His resurrection (16:8-11; cf. Acts 2:25-31), in His ascension (68:18; cf. Hebrews 10:12-13) and in His Second Coming (50:1-6; cf. 1 Thessalonians 4:16; 2 Peter 3:10). He is the shepherd of His people (23; 80:1; cf. John 10:11), the Son of David (78:68-72; cf. Matthew 22:41-46; Psalm 132:11; cf. Matthew 1:1), the Son of Man (8:4; cf. Hebrews 2:6; Matthew 8:20) and the redeemer of God's elect (25:22; 26:11; 130:7-8).

William Balfour (1821-1895), minister of Holyrood Free Church, Edinburgh, speaking in 1880, was surely correct when he said, with reference to Christian truths in the Psalms: 'The question is, Are they there? If we are sure of that, as we certainly are, then it must be our own fault if we do not find them. We must have failed to get into the spirit of the Psalm; and if so, the remedy is not to be found in providing a hymn or hymns in which mention is made of these truths, in so many words, but rather in seeking the Spirit of adoption, without whom the most evangelical hymns ever written will not enable us to praise God aright, and with whom, the Psalms will furnish the richest and most inexhaustible material for praising God.'

All this could be enlarged. The fact is, however, that there is no evidence that references to song in the New Testament refer to anything but to the Psalms of Scripture. No warrant can possibly be taken from these for the adoption of non-inspired compositions. As Professor Macgregor put it so straightforwardly: 'There is no visible case in which with the sanction of God any congregation ever sang a song of merely human inspiration.'

The Psalms are productive of Biblical piety

It has already been mentioned that a Church's song will one way or another influence the piety of the worshippers. With the best will in the world, the singing of hymns of merely human composition - uninspired hymns - will tend to produce a piety no deeper than that of the human author. The piety will reflect his grasp of the truth. And that may be good as far as it goes. However Biblical it may be, it will still fall short of the piety and devotion reflected in the Psalms. For the Psalmists experienced the direct and powerful intervention of God's Spirit in their lives. This ensured that they were the possessors of the reality and power of God's truth in the fullest sense. As a result, the type of piety flowing from a use of the Psalms in worship will be a devotion based entirely on the knowledge and faith, and the reality and power, of the truth of God.

Is it not an evidence of a prevailing shallowness in modern Christianity that the Psalms have largely disappeared from use in the devotions of the Church in general? Whatever experience is being promoted through the hymns, this will not compare with the devotional experience based on the praise materials of divine inspiration, as applied by the Holy Spirit. However attractive songs may be on a human level, they are not thus rendered more palatable to the unsaved person, who in Biblical terms is dead to spiritual realities (cf. 1 Corinthians 2:14; Ephesians 2:1-6). It is when the Spirit of God, who inspired the Psalms, regenerates a person, and makes that person a new creation in Christ (2 Corinthians 5:17), that he or she begins to understand the Psalms in deeply personal terms, not least as songs which speak of Christ, and begins to reflect the experiences of men in whom the Spirit worked directly and powerfully.

Whilst this might be equally argued about hymns, the point is that the Psalms, being the fruit of divine inspiration, must in the nature of the case tend to produce a Biblical piety in a way uninspired materials never can.

The Psalms can be sung without reservation

What makes Psalm singing different from praying and preaching? Each, of course, must have its separate Biblical warrant. But if you allow 'freedom' in praying and preaching, why not also in singing? For the reason that 'This is one part of the service for which a prescribed form is necessary as more than one person joins in utterance at once, and so it must be a form in which all can be expected to join without reservation.'

This is an important point. By providing the Church with the Book of Psalms, the Lord has thereby prevented one preacher or congregation or denomination from coming between a person's conscience and his God in the matter of what he sings, so that his conscience takes the Word of God only as its rule. Because the best of men are but sinful men at best, it is only Biblical materials of praise which may be sung without any reservation in a gathered congregation.

The Psalms encourage the unity of the Church

The adoption of non-inspired materials for praise creates problems for the unity of the Church. It may be illustrated in this way: A leader of the worship announces a hymn (non-canonical variety). Am I bound to sing it? No. Is it a sin for me not to sing it? No, after all it is not the Word of God. But how can the unity of the congregation in its act of sung praise be preserved if all do not sing it? On the other hand, take a psalm (canonical song). The leader gives this out. Am I obliged to sing this? Well, I would have no reason not to.

"Hugh Martin said this in 1872: 'The psalms are the grand Catholic hymnal: and the singing of them provides for Christian union for the perfect Catholicity.'"

Would it be a sin for me not to sing? If I were able to sing, the answer must be, yes. The praise of the sanctuary, especially where participation is involved (as in singing), is to be expressive of the unity of the Church (congregation). Using psalms only cannot disrupt this. Only the psalms of Scripture can *always* be truly ecumenical. Only the psalms of Scripture can be sung without any possible qualms of conscience over the words, expressions, experiences, or theology used, properly understood.

Hugh Martin (1822-1885) said this in 1872: 'The psalms are the grand Catholic hymnal: and the singing of them provides for Christian union for the perfect Catholicity ... If Christ Jesus were bodily present as at the Synagogue in Nazareth would you give him other than his own psalms to lead you in singing? - his own psalms in that they are composed by himself: and his own psalms, in that his soul sang them, with grace in his heart unto the Lord, in the days of his flesh. You maintain communion with him, and he with you, wherein the praises of the sanctuary you sing his psalms. You may think your hymns are in accordance with his word: but the psalms are his very word itself.'

The Psalms should be restored in Christian worship

This amounts to a plea to the Christian Church at large. In his admirable brief work, *The Psalms - Prayer Book of the Bible*, Dietrich Bonhoeffer had this to say: 'A Christian community without the Psalter has lost an incomparable treasure, and by taking it back into use will recover resources it never dreamed it had.' Resources. Spiritual resources. These are materials that moulded the Christian piety of generations - on Biblical lines. In the development of the Church over the past one hundred years or so the Psalms of Scripture have all but disappeared from the formal worship of God in so many Churches. It is our conviction that there needs to be a return to the Psalms in the praises of God. Not only is the Psalter a divinely inspired and appointed collection of God-breathed psalms, hymns and songs, it is also expressive of every aspect of Christian experience and is perfectly balanced theologically. Of course such a return will mean an adjustment of attitudes: a reformation of our singing. But the return will be worthwhile and joyous.

Dr. Henry Cooke of Belfast made this moving plea - a plea, we would suggest, with continuing relevance in the area of worship, - 'While I set not up my own convictions as a rule or measure of the consciences of others, I cannot fail to pity those who can find, as they assert, so little of Christ in the inspired psalmody of the Bible, that they must seek and employ an uninspired psalmody as exhibiting Him more fully. Our Lord Himself found Himself in the psalms - (Luke xxiv. 44, 45) - and thereby "opened His disciples' understanding, that they might understand the Scriptures". Surely what was clearest light to *their* eyes, should be light to *ours*. And, truly, I believe, there is one view of Christ - and that not the least important to the tired and troubled believer - that can be discovered only in the Book of Psalms - I mean His inward life.... The most pious productions of uninspired men are a shallow stream - the Psalms are an unfathomable and shoreless ocean.'

There is nothing more important than the worship of God. The continuing challenge for the Church today, in this matter of how and with what it ought to worship God, is simply that the truth should have its way, however much that may cause recently developed traditions and practices to be overturned and reformed. The modern Church must be willing to let the truth have its way, specifically in this matter of song and the place of the Psalms in worship. What is the Lord's song? It is the song He has given, that He has appointed and provided in His Word.

> O come, let us sing to the Lord:
> come, let us every one
> A joyful noise make to the Rock
> of our salvation.
>
> Let us before His presence come
> with praise and thankful voice;
> Let us sing psalms to Him with grace,
> and make a joyful noise.
> (Psalm 95:1-2, *1650 Psalter*)

FURTHER READING

Beeke, Joel R. and Selvaggio, Anthony T. (Editors), *Sing a New Song*, Grand Rapids, 2010.

    Among the best of a increasing number of books seeking to recover, reclaim or rediscover Psalm-singing in the modern Church. Excellent!

Begg, James, *Anarchy in Worship*, Edinburgh, 1875.

    This small work (48pp) has been reproduced in recent years. It deals with innovations in worship in the context of late nineteenth century Scottish Presbyterianism.

Binnie, William, *The Psalms: Their History, Teachings, and Use*, London, 1886.

    A book which stands alone. Not only full of excellent comment and scholarship from a conservative viewpoint, but this book also provides a fine overview of the Psalter and its Christian use.

Blaikie, Alexander, *A Catechism on Praise*, James Begg Society, 1997.

    Blaikie was a pastor in the Associate Reformed Presbyterian Church, Boston. A useful brief work first published in 1854.

Bonar, A. A., *Christ and His Church in the Book of Psalms*, Stoke on Trent, 2001.

    First published in 1859, this is a superb book which effectively brings out in brief compass, and not in an overstrained way, the Christology of the Psalter. Says Bonar: 'The Psalms are for all ages alike - not more for David than for us.'

Bushell, Michael, *Songs of Zion. The Biblical Basis for Exclusive Psalmody*, Norfolk Press, 2011

    Originally a Master's thesis, this is the most comprehensive and scholarly treatment of 'exclusive Psalmody' in the modern era.

Church, Francis (Ed.), *The True Psalmody*, Edinburgh, 1888.

    A combined effort from ministers and elders of the Reformed and United Presbyterian Churches of Philadelphia.

Gibson, James, *Public Worship of God: Its Authority and Modes*, Glasgow, 1869.

> The work of a Free Church Professor within the context of discussion on the issue in Scottish Presbyterianism.

Kerr, James, McDonald, John, *The Voice of His Praise*, James Begg Society, 1999.

> Reprint of four tracts first issued by the Reformed Presbyterian Church of Scotland, c.1880.

LeFebvre, Michael, *Singing the Songs of Jesus*, Christian Focus, 2010.

> An interesting and powerful argument for the use of Psalms as Christ-centred sung praise.

McNaugher, John (Ed.), *The Psalms in Worship*, Still Waters Revival Books, 1992.

> This comprises a reprint of a volume of Convention Papers on the place of Psalms in Worship, produced by the United Presbyterian Church of North America in 1907. Outstanding.

Psalm Singers' Conference, Belfast, 1903.

> Conference papers covering every aspect of Psalm singing with contributors from the U.S.A. and Europe.

Ramsay, M.C., *Purity of Worship*, Presbyterian Church of Eastern Australia, 1968.

> An excellent 47-page booklet, concise but comprehensive.

RPCNA, *The Biblical Doctrine of Worship*, Reformed Presbyterian Church of North America, 1973.

> An enormously useful Symposium. In some ways an updated version of the Psalm-Singers' Conference publication of 1903.

Smith, Frank J. and Lachman, David C. (Eds.), *Worship in the Presence of God*, Greenville, South Carolina, 1992.

> A thought-provoking and wide-ranging contemporary collection of essays on the nature, elements and historic views and practice of worship.

Songs of the Spirit

Ward, Rowland S., *Psalm-Singing in Scripture and History*, Melbourne, 1992.

A doctrinal and historical study. Particularly useful for the historical overview covering many Churches and countries.

Williamson, G. I., *The Singing of Psalms in the Worship of God*, Belfast, 1972.

A superb little booklet succinctly covering the principles involved.

Chapter V was published in an earlier form by Knox Press in 1994, and by Crown and Covenant Publications in 2003. It is republished here in an updated form by kind permission.

Rev. John W. Keddie retired recently as minister of the Bracadale congregation of the Free Church of Scotland (Continuing), and serves as Lecturer in Church History and Church Principles in the Free Church Seminary, Inverness.

VI.

Therapeutic Praise

David Murray

Despite hundreds of new Christian songs, of every possible genre, being composed every year, the ancient Psalms are experiencing somewhat of a revival. Why?

I believe the main reason is their therapeutic value; in a day of so many disordered emotions, worshippers are discovering how the Psalms minister so powerfully to their emotional lives.

The Psalms balance Divine revelation and human emotion
Some Christian songs are emotionally stirring, but have little theological content; the heart is engaged, but not the mind. Over-reacting to this, some have composed songs that are full of theological facts, but do not engage the worshipper's feelings. They are more like sung sermons.

The Psalms strike an inspired balance of doxological theology and theological doxology; they combine the objective with the subjective in perfect proportions. Time and again we read, "Praise the Lord **for...**" followed by reasons and motivations for this praise. God is declared and described, but always to stir up our hearts and interact with Him through His self-revelation.

The Psalms express the full range of human emotions

The Psalms contain an incomparably rich mixture of extreme and varied emotions: grief and joy, doubt and confidence, loneliness and fellowship, despair and hope, fear and courage, defeat and victory, complaint and praise, etc.

Is it any wonder that Calvin called the Psalms 'an Anatomy of all Parts of the Soul'? As he explained: 'There is not an emotion of which anyone can be conscious that is not here represented as in a mirror. Or rather, the Holy Spirit has here drawn to life all the griefs, sorrows, fears, doubts, hopes, cares, perplexities, in short, all the distracting emotions with which the minds of men are wont to be agitated'.

The Psalms paint a realistic portrayal of Christian emotions

The Psalms do not portray the Christian life as victory upon victory. Derek Thomas has pointed out that because a lot of contemporary worship is upbeat and positive, and therefore at odds with what Christians experience in the rest of their week, it produces a disconnect that eventually leads to cynicism and a loss of assurance.

But when we turn to the Psalms, we find bold and bald honesty. Although the strong expressions of stark reality can initially jar our refined ears, we are soon relieved to find kindred spirits who helpfully express what we often think, feel, and experience in our messy daily lives.

The Psalms open a welcome outlet for our painful emotions

Have you ever sung about assurance while being full of doubt? Have you ever sung about joy when feeling depressed? Me too. And it's horrible, isn't it? Why can't I sing what I really feel? With the Psalms you can! Some allow us to express doubt and even despair (e.g. Psalm 88); others help us describe our struggles with providence (e.g. Ps. 73); still others guide us in explaining our battles with depression (e.g. Pss. 42, 78).

The Psalms open the pressure valve of our hearts and direct us in how to articulate our most painful emotions. We don't need to bottle them up or deny them. Instead God has inspired songs to admit them and let them out. As someone said: 'What a relief! I can sing what's really on my mind and heart, and God provides me

> "The Psalms open the pressure valve of our hearts and direct us in how to articulate our most painful emotions. We don't need to bottle them up or deny them. Instead God has inspired songs to admit them and let them out"

with words to rightly express these emotions. The Psalms reach in to find these emotions and then reach upwards to God with them.'

The Psalms call for the transformation of our emotions

The Psalms not only permit us to 'vent' our emotions, but also call for their transformation. We are not left to wallow in our feelings, but are shown how to move from fear to courage, from sorrow to joy, from anger to peace, and from despair to hope. The painful starting point is legitimate; but it's only a starting point. The end-point of emotional healing must be kept in view, and moved towards with the help of Psalmist's guiding hand.

The Psalms summon us to sympathetic emotion

As a rebellious teenager, I often sat in my Psalm-singing church wondering why I was singing words that had no relevance to me whatsoever. Why sing about sorrow, when I was perfectly happy? Or, some Sundays, why sing about joy when I feel so depressed about my life?

Well of course, such is the mindset of a self-centred teenager. But when God saves us, we begin to look a little beyond ourselves and to realize that while I may not feel these things, others certainly do. The Psalms call me to weep with those who weep, and to rejoice with those who rejoice, no matter if I feel exactly the opposite. They remind me of the emotional diversity of the body of Christ and invite me to share in the sufferings and successes of others. They turn me inside out.

The Psalms supply an emotional stimulus to righteous living

I have been trying to emphasize the emotional engagement and stimulus of the Psalms. However, ultimately, the Psalms use the emotional energy they generate to stimulate practical obedience. Notice how many 'wisdom' Psalms are interspersed throughout the Psalter, setting forth the path of obedience for the stirred up and energized worshipper. Emotional transformation must result in life transformation.

Rev. Dr. David P. Murray is the minister of the Grand Rapids, Michigan, congregation of the Free Reformed Church, and also serves as Professor of Old Testament and Practical Theology at Puritan Reformed Theological Seminary, Grand Rapids, Michigan.

VII.

Is the Psalter Enough?
The Sufficiency of the Book of Psalms
for the Praise of God Today

David Silversides

One of the most frequent objections today to the exclusive use of the Psalms in worship is the question of adequacy. Can the Psalter be regarded as sufficient for the use of the New Testament church, in view of the fact that it was written in the Old Testament period, and that we now have the benefit of the record of redemption accomplished by Christ and the exposition of that event in the Scriptures of the New Testament? It is argued, How can it be right to be confined to the use of a Biblical Psalter that was written, albeit by inspiration of God, in the Old Testament when we now live in the New Testament age.

The argument continues: Either the psalms need to be paraphrased or altered so they may fit in with the New Testament worship, as Isaac Watts maintained, or alternatively that we sing them as they stand, but that on their own they are insufficient and need to be supplemented by uninspired hymns written by godly men who have lived since the New Testament age began. In other words, so it is contended, the Biblical psalms must either be altered or supplemented in order to have a full-orbed collection of materials for praise for the church in the New Testament. It is this view that is challenged here.

I. Important Facts About the Psalms

Firstly, the Psalms are infallibly inspired by God. This should be obvious but needs to be spelled out. We ought to be afraid to criticize any part of the Word of God, including the Book of Psalms. Sometimes in their zeal to oppose exclusive psalmody, men have said things about the Psalms that, on calmer reflection, they must surely realize should never be said about any part of the Word of God. The Psalms are breathed out by God. They are infallible and without error.

When Psalm 95:7-11 is quoted in Hebrews 3:7-8, the words of the Psalm are attributed to the Spirit of God as we read, ' *Wherefore (as the Holy Ghost saith, To day if ye will hear his voice, Harden not your hearts, as in the provocation, in the day of temptation in the wilderness.*' This means that the songs in the Psalter are Spiritual in the highest possible sense.

When we turn to Ephesians 5:19, '*Speaking to yourselves in psalms and hymns and spiritual songs, singing and making melody in your heart to the Lord;*' those of you familiar with the exclusive psalmody position will know that the terms '*psalms*', '*hymns*' and '*songs*' are terms, all three of which (in their Hebrew equivalent and the very words themselves in the Greek translation of the Old Testament) are used in the titles of the Psalms, in the content of the Psalms, and in the content of the Old Testament outside the Book of Psalms, to describe the Book of Psalms. A more detailed argument can be found elsewhere, but sufficient to say for the purpose of this paper, that we regard psalms, hymns and songs as three terms all referring to the book of psalms.

The original word order is 'psalms and hymns and songs spiritual' (*psalmois kai humnois kai odais pneumatikais*) so that the word 'spiritual' could refer simply to the songs, or it could qualify all three terms: spiritual psalms, hymns and songs. What does the word spiritual mean, even if it's only referring to the songs? The answer is in verse 18: '*And be not drunk with wine, wherein is excess; but be filled with the Spirit; Speaking to yourselves in psalms and hymns and spiritual songs*'. The word 'spirit' is *pneumti* (v.18) and the word 'spiritual' (v.19) is *pneumatikais*. Just as in English, so also in Greek, the word 'spirit' and 'spiritual' are essentially one word, one being the adjective form of the other, which is a noun. In verse 18 it

> "One of the means of being filled with the Holy Spirit is to sing those songs that are breathed out by the Holy Spirit. The contents of the Psalter are of the Spirit of God in the highest possible sense of being given and indited word for word by the Holy Spirit"

is quite clear the Spirit in view is none other than the Holy Spirit and therefore one of the means of being filled with the Holy Spirit is to sing those songs that are breathed out by the Holy Spirit. Spiritual songs are songs of the Holy Spirit, not in some vague sense of having something to do with the human spirit or 'spiritual things', which term we tend to use in rather a loose sense. The contents of the Psalter are of the Spirit of God in the highest possible sense of being given and indited word for word by the Holy Spirit.

Moreover, this means that the Book of Psalms are the Word of Christ. Note the parallel passage in Colossians 3:16, *Let the word of Christ dwell in you richly in all wisdom; teaching and admonishing one another in psalms and hymns and spiritual songs, singing with grace in your hearts to the Lord.* Here the practice of singing these psalms and hymns and spiritual songs is an aspect of letting *the word of Christ dwell in you richly in all wisdom.* The Psalms are the Word of Christ in the highest possible sense. They were given by the Spirit of Christ, they speak of Christ (Luke 24:44) and they were also sung by the Lord Jesus Christ in the days of His flesh. The Lord Jesus didn't sing some composition of a mere man. He sang the Psalms given by God.

The distinction between infallible revelation and that which is written by good, but fallible, men must be rigorously maintained. No amount of sentiment or tradition must blur that. The Psalms were inspired by God. Sometimes people say, 'Well weren't these good men, in a sense, inspired by God.' No, they were not: not Isaac Watts, Toplady or Doddridge or anyone else since the completion of the canon of Holy Scripture. We do not say they were not godly men and that the Spirit of God gave them understanding in the truth, but their productions were not the inspired Word of God, otherwise they would need to be included in the Bible. We do not believe in inspiration outside of the Scriptures, whether we have in view the Pope in Rome, or a charismatic pseudo-apostle, or even godly men who wrote poems that they thought should be used in the worship of God. The difference between the Word of God and the word even of godly men must be rigorously maintained.

Secondly, the names of Christ do appear in the Psalms. The Hebrew Old Testament name 'Jehovah' is normally rendered LORD in our English Authorised Version. In the Greek translation of the Old Testament, known as the Septuagint and often quoted by the apostles, the word *kurios* is used to translate *Jehovah* when the Old Testament is being quoted in the New. It is also the word that is constantly used when the New Testament speaks of the Lord (*kurios*) Jesus Christ. The Hebrew Jehovah appears constantly in the Book of Psalms and sometimes very clearly referring to the

Lord Jesus Christ. For example, Psalm 102:21-24 refers to the LORD (Jehovah) and yet verses 25-27 are quoted in Hebrews 1:10-12 as applying to the Lord Jesus Christ. So when the Book of Psalms speaks of Jehovah, we would be wrong to assume that there is no reference to the Lord Jesus Christ.

Likewise, the name Jesus means *saviour* and this term and especially *salvation* appear in many of the Psalms (Psalms= 3:8, 9:14, 13:5 etc.).

Again, the name *Christ* appears in the Book of Psalms. Psalm 2:2 is quoted in the Greek rendering in Acts 4:25, 26 '*Who by the mouth of thy servant David hast said, Why did the heathen rage, and the people imagine vain things? The kings of the earth stood up, and the rulers were gathered together against the Lord, and against his Christ*'. Christ is simply the English form of the Greek *Christos*, which is the equivalent of Messiah in Hebrew, meaning 'anointed'.

The names of Christ do appear in the Psalms.

Thirdly, the Psalms are much quoted in the New Testament. In Hebrews 1 and 2, where we are shown that God has spoken in these last days by His Son, we get quotations from Psalms 45, 110, 102, 104, 22, 8 and 22. Likewise, the apostles in the Book of Acts, in preaching, make very full use of the book of the book of Psalms. In actual fact if you were to count up either direct quotations from the Psalms, or the use of the language of the Psalms in the New Testament, you will find there are some 300 places where either the Psalter is quoted or the language of the Psalter is used in the New Testament. I would recommend the book *Make His Praise Glorious* by Roy Mohon, p.25, for a fuller treatment of this point, and indeed this work offers a fuller exposition of a number of matters addressed in the present article.

Fourthly, the Psalter's prophecies concerning the sufferings of Christ are in the past tense. Sometimes the objection is raised that all that is said about Christ in the Psalms is prophetic and refers to the future. This is true in that they are prophetic because it was written before the event, but it is not true that all is written as in the future.

'Many bulls have compassed me: strong bulls of Bashan have beset me round. They gaped upon me with their mouths, as a ravening and a roaring lion. I am poured out like water, and all my bones are out of joint: my heart is like wax; it is melted in the midst of my bowels. My strength is dried up like a potsherd; and my tongue cleaveth to my jaws; and

"God has given us a book of praise in the Old Testament, ideally suited for the people of God in the New"

thou hast brought me into the dust of death. For dogs have compassed me: the assembly of the wicked have inclosed me: they pierced my hands and my feet. I may tell all my bones: they look and stare upon me. They part my garments among them, and cast lots upon my vesture' (Psalm 22:12-18).

This is undoubtedly speaking of the Lord Jesus. It is partly in the past tense and partly in the present. The point to be grasped is that the Lord used David's sufferings for the truth's sake, as the providentially ordained occasion of his prophesying far beyond himself to the sufferings of the coming Christ. Although prophetic, it is written not as something in the future but as something presently happening or that has already happened.

'Reproach hath broken my heart; and I am full of heaviness: and I looked for some to take pity, but there was none; and for comforters, but I found none. They gave me also gall for my meat; and in my thirst they gave me vinegar to drink' (Psalm 69:20-21).

Although the Psalms contain prophecy concerning the sufferings of Christ, much that is written about Christ is not written as something in the future. This is quite important because it indicates that, in the plan of God, He was giving in the Old Testament a book of praise for the use of His people after the coming of Christ and fully adequate even, for example, at the Lord's table when remembering the death of Christ in the past. When we come to the Lord's Table and we sing these psalms, we do not consider there is any anomaly at all. We are not remembering what took place in the past but singing of it as if it is something yet to happen in the future. God has given us a book of praise in the Old Testament, ideally suited for the people of God in the New.

Fifthly, the Psalter has no Divinely-inspired supplement in the New Testament. God provided His church in the Old Testament with a perfectly pure book of praise. If that book were inadequate, would we not expect that the Lord would provide a New Testament supplement of inspired songs. But there is none. There is no New Testament equivalent of the Book of Psalms. This is very significant. Is the New Testament, in order to have a supposedly more adequate book of praise, to have a lower standard of purity of content in its songs of praise than the church in the Old Testament? Surely not! If the infallible Psalter of the Old Testament was really inadequate, God would surely have given us a New Testament book of Psalms.

Sixthly, there is no promised gift of hymn composition in the New Testament Church. Even if we could bring ourselves to accept the possibility of the inspired Psalter having been intended to be supplemented by the compositions of uninspired men in the New Testament church, we would expect some gift to be promised to this end, would we not? But you may say that it is obvious from the fact that there are good men who wrote sound hymns that the Lord did make such provision for the supplementing of the Old Testament Psalter. But this is not obvious at all. The presence of an ability to do something, on its own, never justifies the inclusion of that thing in the worship of God.

If there are people who are good at art, do we allow art into the worship of God? If someone is good at sculpture, shall that be included? Do we allow that the existence of an ability to do something, and the claim that it is intended to glorify God in its use, is an adequate basis for bringing that activity into the worship of God? Roman Catholicism has no difficulty with this, of course, since all activities can and should be brought under the jurisdiction of the 'church' (i.e. the papacy) whether art, sculpture or music – all should be under church control along with the government of nations, education, healthcare etc. And those abilities that can find expression in worship, the church has the right to incorporate in its services.

But this is not Protestant teaching nor is it Biblical teaching. All of life is to be lived under the Word of God and for the honour of Christ, but not all of life is to be governed by the church as an organization. The organized church has limited functions appointed by its Head and carried out within the limits prescribed by Him. The fact that there have been men of poetic ability and theological orthodoxy that can produce poetic verse, does not mean it should be brought into the worship of God, unless we can show from the Scriptures that the ascended Christ has promised such a gift for that purpose. Will we find this when we search the Scriptures? There is no mention of hymn composers preparing pieces for the people of God to use in their worship.

The argument for exclusive Psalmody does not rest on the idea that every part of New Testament worship must be confined to inspired words. We do say, however, that there is a promised provision for each part of worship. When it comes to what should be read in worship, we have the infallible Scriptures. When it comes to the preaching of the Word, preachers are not infallible but we do have the promise of the gift of teachers from the ascended Christ (1 Corinthians 12:29; Ephesians 4:11). When it comes to prayer, we have the promise of the help of the Holy

Spirit (Romans 8:26). When it comes to singing praise, there is no promise of a continuing ordinary gift of hymn composition, but there is an infallible, inspired book of 150 compositions provided and appointed to be sung in the praise of God.

Seventhly, many who have stood for the truth under severe trial have found the Psalter adequate. Not every hero of the faith was committed to exclusive psalmody but many were and many sang the Psalms, even in the face of suffering and death, and found them fully adequate. The Reformers sang the Psalms; some in the time of the Reformation who faced being burned at the stake sang the Psalms, even as the flames were increasing. When the Covenanters stood on the scaffold waiting to be hanged, they sang the Psalms. Margaret Wilson sang from Psalm 25 when she was about to be drowned in the waters of Solway for Christ's cause in Scotland in 1685. None of these martyrs felt let down because they only had the Psalms to sing. The whole Westminster Assembly, during their special days of prayer and fasting sang the Psalms. No one complained that they were inadequate for New Testament believers. Does any inadequacy, in fact, lie with us? The Book of Psalms is perfect; it comes from God. The problem has to be with us.

Eighthly, God's provision is always sufficient. The whole argument from the alleged insufficiency of the Psalter is no argument at all. The question is quite simply, what has God appointed? If the answer is that God has appointed the Book of Psalms, it must be sufficient. Any inadequacy must be in our appreciation of the Psalter and we need to change and seek grace to that end. Those who are used to singing hymns may find it hard to abandon them because one does get attached to them. The answer does not lie in denying the truth of exclusive psalmody, but in seeking grace to properly appreciate the Psalms. When this is given, the hymns will not be missed after all. What God has provided is always best.

II. A survey of the contents of the Book of Psalms

Let us briefly survey the scope of the contents of the Psalter.

a) The Word of God.

What does the Psalter say about the word of God? Here we have what the Psalter says about the Word of God.

The purity of God's Word:

'The law of the LORD is perfect, converting the soul: the testimony of the LORD is sure, making wise the simple. The statutes of the LORD are right, rejoicing the heart: the commandment of the LORD is pure, enlightening the eyes. The fear of the LORD is clean, enduring for ever: the judgments of the LORD are true and righteous altogether. More to be desired are they than gold, yea, than much fine gold: sweeter also than honey and the honeycomb. Moreover by them is thy servant warned: and in keeping of them there is great reward' (Psalm 19:7-11).

The Sufficiency of God's Word:

'Therefore I esteem all thy precepts concerning all things to be right; and I hate every false way' (Psalm 119:128).

b) About God

The Psalter tells us that God is a Spirit unlike the false gods of the heathen (Psalm 115:1-11). He is omnipresent (Psalm 139:1-18). He is infinite (Psalm 147:5), eternal (Psalm 90:2) and unchangeable (Psalm 102:26-27). The Psalter tells of God's wisdom and His power (Psalm 147:5), His holiness (Psalm 99:9), justice (Psalm 11:6-7), goodness (Psalms 145:9 & 36:7) and truth (Psalm 31:5).

c) God's Works of Creation, Providence and Redemption

The Psalter speaks of God' s works of creation (Psalm 104

goes through the six days of creation) and providence (Psalm 33:9-11). The Psalter speaks very clearly about man's sin (Psalms 14 & 53). The doctrine of election is in the Book of Psalms (Psalm 33:12; Psalm 65:4).

The Psalter says plenty about Christ the Redeemer: His Deity (Psalm 45:6, c.f. Heb 1:8-9), and His incarnation and active obedience (Psalm 40:7-8, c.f. Heb 10:5-9).

Christ is our **Prophet** (Psalm 40:9, c.f. Heb 2:12; the great congregation is not simply the Church of David's day, except by way of foretaste; rather it is speaking of the whole Church of God, among whom Christ, the Son of David, is the firstborn among many brethren).

Christ is our **Priest** (Psalm 110:4), suffering for sin (Psalm 69:20-21, c.f. Matt 27:34 & 48; Psalm 22:1, c.f. Matt 27:35; v.7-8 c.f. Matt 27: 39-43; v.16, c.f. Matt 27:35; v.18, c.f. Matt 27:35). Although we refer here to the verses that are quoted in the New Testament, other verses, in Psalm 22 for example, give more details of the inner sufferings of Christ than anything to be found elsewhere in the Scriptures.

The completeness of Christ's sufferings is expressed in Psalm 31:5 (c.f. Luke 23:46) and Psalm 22:31 ('...*that he hath done this*') which Christ appears to have in mind when He cried, '*It is finished*' (John 19:30).

Christ is our **King.** His burial, resurrection, ascension and

> "Christ is our **King.** His burial, resurrection, ascension and exaltation to reign at the Father's right hand are all found in the Book of Psalms"

exaltation to reign at the Father's right hand are all found in the Book of Psalms (Ps. 16:8-11; 68:16-20; 110:1). These verses are all quoted in the New Testament (Acts 2:24-32; Eph 4:7-12; Acts 2:34-36) as referring to Christ, and as explaining His continuing to 'do and teach' (Acts 1:1-2) from the Father's right hand, and bestowing gifts among men for that end.

Christ's mediatorial kingship over all, in executing God's decree in providence and His kingship over the Church in the kingdom of grace, is found in Psalms 110:1; 104:4 (c.f. Heb.1:7); 2:6-12 (c.f. Acts 4:25-18); 89:20-28; 22:25-31 etc. The theme of Psalm 45 is the bridegroom taking His bride, speaking of Christ and the Church. Christ the King who is also the Husband and Head of the Church, Who loved the Church and gave Himself for it.

Thus we have Christ as Prophet, Priest and King, that is the King who has power over all things, who ought to be acknowledged as King over all men and nations and who is the King and Head of the Church.

Redemption applied through the covenant of grace is abundantly set forth in the Book of Psalms.

Psalm 95:7 takes up the Covenant theme found in both Old Testament and New, *'For he is our God; and we are the people of his pasture, and the sheep of his hand. To day if ye will hear his voice'* (c.f. Genesis 17:7; 2 Corinthians 6:16; Revelation 21:7).

'But the mercy of the LORD is from everlasting to everlasting upon them that fear him, and his righteousness unto children's children; To such as keep his covenant, and to those that remember his commandments to do them' (Psalm 103:17-18).

'All the paths of the LORD are mercy and truth unto such as keep his covenant and his testimonies' (Psalm 25:10),

'The secret of the LORD is with them that fear him; and he will shew them his covenant' (Psalm 25:14).

Effectual calling is set forth: *'Thy people shall be willing in the day of thy power, in the beauties of holiness from the womb of the morning: thou hast the dew of thy youth'* (Psalm 110:3).

Conviction of sin is described: *'When I kept silence, my bones waxed old through my roaring all the day long. For day and night thy hand was heavy upon me: my moisture is turned into the drought of summer'* (Psalm 32:3-4).

Confession of sin, repentance and faith towards Christ: *'Create in me a clean heart, O God; and renew a right spirit within me'* (Psalm 51:10).

' I intreated thy favour with my whole heart: be merciful unto me according to thy word. I thought on my ways, and turned my feet unto thy testimonies. I made haste, and delayed not to keep thy commandment' (Psalm 119:58-60).

'If thou, LORD, shouldest mark iniquities, O Lord, who shall stand? But there is forgiveness with thee, that thou mayest be feared' (Psalm 130:3-4).

Justification is set forth: *'I acknowledged my sin unto thee, and mine iniquity have I not hid. I said, I will confess my transgressions unto the LORD; and thou forgavest the iniquity of my sin'* (Psalm 32:5). Verses 1-2 are quoted by the Apostle Paul in Romans 4 and give the objective aspect, forgiveness and peace with God, while verse 5 gives the subjective, the enjoyment of the peace of God in the soul. See also Psalm 130:4,7-8.

Equally, we see Adoption: *'Like as a father pitieth his children, so the LORD pitieth them that fear him'* (Psalm 103:13).

The doctrine of sanctification, through the truth of God, is found throughout Psalm 119. Our dependence upon the Spirit of God to enlighten us, and to quicken us in the truth of God, is also found in this Psalm (e.g. v.33-35, 169-176).

The place of trial in the Christian life as a means of sanctification is set before us: *'It is good for me that I have been afflicted; that I might learn thy statutes'* (Psalm 119:71).

Similarly, we see persecution in the experience of the people of God: *'For thou, O God, hast proved us: thou hast tried us, as silver is tried. Thou broughtest us into the net; thou laidst affliction upon our loins. Thou hast caused men to ride over our heads; we went through* fire and through water: but thou broughtest us out into a wealthy place' (Psalm 66:10).

'For, lo, thine enemies make a tumult: and they that hate thee have lifted up the head. They have taken crafty counsel against thy people, and consulted against thy hidden ones. They have said, Come, and let us cut them off from being a nation; that the name of Israel may be no more in remembrance' (Psalm 83:2-4).

> "By the Spirit of God, blessing the singing of this part of His Word, which He gave for singing, we can expect to be directed to right thoughts of God"

Likewise Psalm 129 deals with persecution as a part of the experience of the people of God, 'Many a time have they afflicted me from my youth...' (Psalm 129:1).

The Church and zeal for its worship is included in Psalm 84, 87 & 122 and its unity in Psalm 133. The revival of The Church's prayer for revival is encouraged in Psalms 67, 126 and 85:5-7 and the promises of great Gospel advance in Psalm 22:27ff; 86:9; 102:13-22; 67:5-7 and 68:31-32.

Psalm 72 takes in the mediatorial dominion of Christ and the advance of the gospel even on the tops of the mountains (i.e. in the most unlikely places to human eyes).

Then the coming of Christ in judgment, we have in Psalm 50, 96 and 98. The new Heavens and a new earth is prophesied in Psalm 102:24-28. The glorification of the people of God is beautifully described in Psalm 73:24; 16:9-11 and 17:15.

We have only roughly skimmed through the contents of

the Psalms but sufficiently, we trust, to show that all the major doctrines of the Word of God find some expression in the Book of Psalms. The order in which we have conducted our brief sketch approximates to the doctrinal outline of the Shorter Catechism. If we consider this Book of Psalms inadequate, one of two things is true.

1. We either do not know them or do not understand them.

2. We have got so attached to uninspired hymns, by way of usage, that we are unable to look at the issue without bias.

III. The Blessings Anticipated From Singing The Psalms

What benefits can we anticipate from singing the Psalms in God's worship?

1. Immediate benefits from the actual singing of them.

Firstly, freedom from error. We can have confidence in the content because it is part of the Word of God. Our consciences need not be burdened as to whether the act of singing them has Divine approval or whether the content is doctrinally sound. There are no bad Psalms. We can look to God to bless His own Word to us.

Secondly, right thoughts of God. By the Spirit of God, blessing the singing of this part of His Word, which He gave for singing, we can expect to be directed to right thoughts of God. How important this is, and who better to tell us what God is like than God Himself?

2. Longer term benefits.

Firstly, if we sing the Psalms, it is the Word of God that gets fastened in our minds. What a great blessing in the time of trial, popularity or the time of death. We need the Word of God Himself at such times. Knowing what some good man thought is not enough.

Secondly, the singing of Psalms contributes to the safety of the

Church. Heretics can bring in heresy without hymns, of course, but hymns have been a fruitful means of bringing false doctrine into the Church. Heretics have not been slow to grasp that a good tune can sweep along the unwary. Augustine writes, *The Donatists make it a matter of reproach against us, that in the Church, we sing with sobriety the divine songs…whereas they inflame the intoxication of their minds by singing psalms of human composition'* (Confessions, ix, 4).

The Psalms set a God-given boundary, to keep out the nonsense. How much we need that today when the Church is being swamped with musical entertainment. Normally sensible, sober and even doctrinally-aware people end up singing the most banal and trivial ditties imaginable because there is no barrier to withstand the flood. Those who think of God, in His greatness and glory, cannot but be troubled at the dumbing down of worship and the onslaught of musical trivia today. The answer is not just to haggle about what we think is best or reverent or sufficiently substantial in content. The answer is God's hymnbook; the Psalter. The rest must go.

Thirdly, the unity of the Church. People see exclusive Psalmody as divisive. The reverse is the case. Psalm-singing is a uniting factor conducive to fulfilling the apostolic injunction, 'That ye may with one mind and one mouth glorify God, even the Father of our Lord Jesus Christ' (Romans 15:6).

Speaking of one of the most conservative non-exclusive psalmody denominations, which has spent far more time and care on the production of its hymnbook than most, G.I. Williamson offers this personal observation,

'*I was present at the Denver Assembly of the Orthodox Presbyterian Church in 1956, when the list of songs was presented to the Assembly for inclusion in the proposed new hymnal. I still remember the fascinating debate about the content of these uninspired hymns. Again and again a delegate would stand up and object to the content – the teaching of such and such an hymn. Often the objections were formidable in my eyes. Yet over and over the objection was denied. I felt that popularity was the overruling factor. But the thing that remains with me is the fact that when men determine the content of the book of praise of the Church of Jesus Christ there can never be a book of praise against which the scruples of conscience will not remain – unless all concern for truth is dead!'* (Trinity Hymnal, a paper by G.I. Williamson in 'The Biblical Doctrine of Worship' pub. Crown & Covenant Publications, Pittsburgh, 1974).

CONCLUSION

When the Church has been most united, exclusive psalmody has been the norm. Hymn singing is a cause of division and a fruit of the individualism sown by division. When was the Church in the British Isles most united? In the Puritan times, the Church was not perfectly united by any means, but far more so than today. They didn't have any problems about what they sang. They could all sing the Psalms. The Westminster Assembly did not agree about everything but they could all sing the Psalms. Here, in the Psalter, is a hymnbook that all can sing from with a clear conscience, knowing that it is without error and tells us only the truth about God and is completely adequate for the Church today. Psalm singing is a uniting ordinance appointed by God and with the promise of His blessing. Let us unite in doing as the Psalmist tells us, *'Sing unto him, sing psalms unto him'* (Psalm 105:2).

Rev. David Silversides is the minister of the Loughbrickland congregation of the Reformed Presbyterian Church of Ireland.

VIII.

Christ's Abiding Presence in the Psalms

Matthew Vogan

Some claim that the Psalms of Scripture are not sufficient for the praise of God in public worship. They assert that the Lord Jesus Christ ought to be mentioned as explicitly as possible in our praise. With this weak objection, they open the door to uninspired hymns. A deeper appreciation of the Psalms should, however, convince us that the Lord Jesus Christ could hardly be more in the Psalms than He is. 'All things must be fulfilled, which were written in the law of Moses, and in the prophets, and in the psalms, concerning Me' (Luke 24:44). The Psalms are indeed full of Christ but, as we shall endeavour to discover, this goes even beyond pointing forward to Christ.

In his valuable book, *Christ's Presence in the Gospel History* (more recently published as *The Abiding Presence*), Hugh Martin shows that the Gospels are not merely a historical record but a means of communion with a living Christ. He observes that no ordinary biography, or even autobiography, concludes with the promise, 'Lo, I am with you alway, even unto the end of the world'

(Matthew 28:20).

The Gospels must be approached with this promise of His presence. 'Take the Gospel record in your hands,' Martin says, 'and you have the means of causing you to realise Christ's presence. The biography then is not dead, the living One lives in it. The presence is not mysterious and vague; for He is present as in the mirror of the biography, and according to the well defined and reflected glory there. The biography is more than biography now, it is – the life of Jesus.' Through the work of the Holy Spirit in the inspiration of Scripture and in the indwelling and illumination of the believer, there is a certain knowledge and true experience of Christ through the infallible Word and living presence.

In the Psalms, we have precisely the same thing. E S McKitrick states that 'the Person of Christ is fully presented in the Psalter, as well as His work. Indeed, it has been asserted, and not without reason, that out of the Psalms one could compile a biography of Jesus.' McKitrick goes on to show that the full range of matters and events associated with the Person and work of Christ are to be found within the Psalms. The Psalms not only unfold the life of Christ; they give us in many instances the very words and thoughts of the Saviour. E S McKitrick writes: 'In these revelations of Jesus in the Psalter, there is this advantage over all others: He speaks mainly in the first person, and tells us His own feelings while working and suffering and dying for our redemption. And these revelations are chiefly in the past tense, as if to indicate that they were intended more for the gospel age than for that in which they were written' ('Christ in the Psalms', in *The Psalms in Worship*, John McNaugher, ed, Pittsburgh, 1907).

We are therefore reading and singing of fulfilments, not merely predictions. It is notable that the Psalms have a prominent and frequent emphasis upon the current position of the Saviour, His mediatorial kingship and His sitting at the right hand of God in heaven. These features of Christ's work are indeed very scarce in collections of uninspired hymns.

R J George also expressed helpfully the fullness of Christ

in the Psalms: 'Christ is the speaker in many of them ... Christ alone is the subject of many of them ... The truth is that no book of the Bible reveals Christ with such fullness as the Book of Psalms, not excepting the Gospel according to John or the Epistle to the Hebrews' (*The Free Presbyterian Magazine*, vol 30, p 288). Henry Cooke writes: 'Truly, I believe, there is one view of Christ – and that not the least important to the tried and troubled believer – that can be discovered only in the Book of Psalms; I mean His inward life. ... The Spirit who "searcheth the deep things of God' has, in the Psalms, laid open the inmost thoughts, sorrows and conflicts of our Lord. The Evangelists faithfully and intelligently depict the sinless Man; the Psalms alone lay open the heart of 'the Man of sorrows'" (*The True Psalmody*, 1861, p 17). When we consider them from this perspective, we might easily be constrained to say that the Gospels are the biography of Christ, but the Psalms His autobiography.

We may go still further, since in singing the Psalms we are taking these very words upon our lips together. Scripture tells us that Christ is specially present and directly participating when the Church is singing praise: 'In the midst of the church will I sing praise unto Thee' (Hebrews 2:12, quoting from Psalm 22). We have the living presence of Christ as we sing His own words concerning Himself in the Psalms. Christ indwells His people and enters into special communion with them through His Word. We must offer our praise in and through Him (Hebrews 13:15). Calvin comments upon the foregoing verse: 'It thus appears that our Lord is the leader of our songs and chief composer of our hymns'.

In *The Abiding Presence*, Martin highlights examples from the days of Christ's time on earth that can be considered in the light of the promised reality of Christ's continued presence with His people. He writes of 'The Temptation, and its perpetual Triumph' and 'The Synagogue and its perpetual Sermon'. We could add another example: 'The Last Supper, and its perpetual Praise' (Mark 14:26). Christ sang a psalm in the midst of His brethren, as a part of the Supper that was being instituted in the world to be observed 'till He come'. He has promised to be with His people 'alway, even to the end of the world' (Matthew 28:20) and He will be specially present in their singing of His Psalms.

Hugh Martin gave a speech to the General Assembly of the Free Church of Scotland defending the exclusive use of the Psalms in praise. In this he emphasises that Christ 'is spiritually present with His people in their worship in the sanctuary. But were He bodily present as in the synagogue of Nazareth, when there was given to Him the book of the prophet Isaiah, would you give Him any other book of song than the book of the Psalms of David? ... Would you give Him other than His own Psalms to lead you in singing – His own Psalms, in that they are composed by Himself; and His own Psalms, in that His soul sang them, with grace in His heart unto the Lord, in the days of His flesh? You maintain communion with Him, and He with you, when, in the praises of the sanctuary, you sing His Psalms.' No wonder that the spiritual singing of praise is frequently spoken of as a duty that resembles the exercises of the saints in heaven in their immediate enjoyment of communion with Christ.

What Martin has written concerning the presence of Christ in the Gospels may be clearly discerned in the Psalms also. Christ's 'own blessed voice speaketh with me in the lively oracles. His own blessed face looks forth upon me from the now-living picture of His biography. By an arrangement that leaves nothing for imagination to attempt, and therefore no room for imagination to misconceive, nothing for sentimentalism to supply, and therefore no scope for sentimentalism to pervert; by an arrangement that leaves me no discretion whatsoever, but calls on me simply to receive the heavenly revelation that is given, *the Lord is Himself with me* – not to my fancy, not to my pious sentiment, but with me verily and in very truth.' It must be His own perfect inspired truth, in order that He 'should enter into it, identify Himself with it, invest Himself with it, make it vital with His living power and vocal with His own personal voice, make it from age to age the dwelling-place of His presence'. It must have 'absolute infallibility, in order that my

Lord be in nothing misrepresented to me . . . a mirror on which no staining breath of human imperfection has been permitted to pass' (*The Abiding Presence*, Knox Press reprint, pp 25-6,57,60).

We need the perfect self-revelation of Christ in His own words in order truly to have communion with Him. We do not need the misplaced imagination and sentimentalism of uninspired hymn writers when we have communion with the person of Christ directly through His own Word in the Psalms. We can then sing the Psalms 'in faith untainted with doubt, in the full assurance of faith, unshackled from the spirit of criticism which man's word continually provokes, yea demands' (Hugh Martin, in *The Free Presbyterian Magazine*, vol 2, p 27). As Henry Cooke expressed it, 'The most pious productions of uninspired men are a shallow stream – the Psalms are an unfathomable and shoreless ocean'. Spiritual singing of the Psalms in this way enables us to go beyond 'conceptions, notions, ideas concerning Him, however true'. 'You deal with Him, and He with you. The true and living Christ, present with you – secretly and subjectively present in you by His Spirit – deals with you. And you in the Spirit deal with the true and living Christ, present with you – ostensibly and objectively present with you – in His own holy Word' (*The True Psalmody*, 1861, pp 17,37).

This is to have the 'Word of Christ dwell in you richly, in all wisdom' (Colossians 3:16). Martin says, 'I can understand how the Word of God should dwell in us richly by singing the Word of God – dwelling on it in solemn, meditative, grave, sweet singing of it, till – to use a Scotch phrase – it seeps into the soul and takes its dwelling there, while in warm emotion of faith the worshipper's spirit in believing song dwells deliberately upon it. Thus it may come to dwell richly in us' (*The Free Presbyterian Magazine*, vol 2, p 25). 'According to our spirituality of mind and in proportion to the vigour and activity of our faith', the Psalms 'are to us the Galleries of the King, replete and lighted up with living and presently subsisting revelations of our Lord' (*The Abiding Presence*, p 61).

They are greatly mistaken who believe that the Psalms must

be set aside on the view that the Lord Jesus Christ ought to be mentioned as explicitly as possible within our praise. When the Psalms are sung, Christ could not be more present in both the content and spiritual reality of the praise. A handful of worshippers singing unaccompanied psalms in an old building might seem contemptible to the carnal assumptions of the world and a worldly church, but there are depths of far greater spiritual reality in the singing than they are able to discern. There are 'the goings of the King' within the sanctuary (Psalm 68:24). The Saviour Himself is present, engaged and drawn to His people, saying, 'Let Me hear thy voice, for sweet is thy voice' (Song of Solomon 2:14).

Faith goes again and again to the Psalms and finds fresh truth and means of grace there, through fresh views of Christ. Martin himself describes this vitality in the religion of the Psalms of David: 'The religion of intense personality and adoring, loving fellowship with God, through a personal and fraternal Mediator, is a religion of inexhaustible resources; of ever-varying experiences; instinct with the charms of fresh, unflagging novelty, and of ceaseless variation; echoing joyfully, in its onward march and history, to the harmonious movement and the continually changing combinations of all honourable affections. Just because of its personality it is so' (*The Abiding Presence*, p 177).

As believers go up from this wilderness leaning upon their Beloved, the Psalms are perfectly suited to be the songs of their pilgrimage (Song of Solomon 8:5). 'The ransomed of the Lord shall return, and come to Zion with songs' (Isaiah 35:10).

Chapter VIII was originally printed in the Free Presbyterian Magazine, August 2013, and is reprinted by kind permission.

Matthew Vogan is a local government project manager, and a ruling elder in the Inverness congregation of the Free Presbyterian Church of Scotland.

IX.

What Should Accompany our Worship of God?
An Argument from Scripture for Unaccompanied Sung Praise

Kenneth Stewart

INTRODUCTION

This case for using musical accompaniment in worship is relatively straightforward. It is usually argued that the use of musical instruments in old covenant worship is enough to justify their use in new covenant worship. The silence of the New Testament should not pose a problem at all. The assumption should be that these instruments were used in the apostolic church too— it's just that they don't happen to be mentioned, that's all.

However, simple as it appears to be, the case does not do full justice to one important issue: the precise nature of the change which took place with the passing of the old covenant – with its priesthood and its worship – and with the advent of the new covenant.

To put it more starkly, let's just see what happens when we substitute *incense and altars* for *musical instruments* in the paragraph above. If you were convinced by the paragraph when you read it, let's see how you feel when we make the change. Here it is:

This case is relatively straightforward. It is usually argued that the use of altars and incense in old covenant worship is enough to warrant our use of them in new covenant worship. The silence of the New Testament should not pose a problem at all. The assumption should be that they were used in the apostolic church too— it's just that they don't happen to be mentioned, that's all.

The case seems equally plausible – and so it would be if we substituted vestments or anointing oil! This goes to show that the case is not as simple as it appears.

For one thing, although there is considerable use of musical accompaniment in worship under the old covenant, there is no evidence anywhere that the organised, regular, corporate worship meetings of Israel ever included the use of musical instruments. If the ordinary weekly worship meetings of the people on their Sabbath in the synagogue *did* include them, their absence in the later synagogue, and indeed the early church, becomes inexplicable.

For another, the New Testament silence is deafening! On the face of it, it constitutes a fairly powerful argument for avoiding their use in new covenant worship altogether. However, it could easily be objected that this amounts to an argument from silence – which is admittedly a precarious form of argument. In other words, the objector could argue that the fact that they are not mentioned in connection with New Testament praise does not, in itself, mean that they were not used. Again, however, the issue is not as simple as that. If worship itself were hardly referred to in the New Testament at all, then it would indeed be perilous to argue the avoidance of musical instruments from silence. However, the New Testament is hardly silent on the issue of worship.

As well as the references to worship throughout the Gospels and the book of Acts, Paul's first letter to the Corinthians has an extensive discussion on worship in chapters 11 through to 14. More to the point, First Timothy is primarily written to give Timothy further guidance on issues primarily to do with worship. A lot of this material is connected with the correction of abuses which had crept into the worship of the church. Knowing the ease with which musical instruments can be abused in such worship, it seems remarkable that not one word is spoken regarding their use or abuse in all this Biblical material!

After all, it is worth bearing in mind that the only reason the use of instrumental accompaniment didn't cause argument under the old covenant lay in the fact that its use was tightly regulated by prophetic authority: the *number* of instruments used, their *kind*, their precise *use* – all this was explicitly stipulated by David in response to the express command of God, as we shall see in a moment.

> "In all the references to worship in the New Testament, it would seem plain that the ordinary, non-ceremonial pattern of worship in the synagogue – with which the Apostles were so familiar – became the established pattern of worship in the Christian church"

All this on its own makes the silence more significant. However, there is more than just the silence. In all the references to worship in the New Testament, it would seem plain that the ordinary, non-ceremonial pattern of worship in the synagogue – with which the Apostles were so familiar – became the established pattern of worship in the Christian church. The evidence for this is overwhelming – not least in the fact that the assembly of Christians is actually referred to as a 'synagogue' in the New Testament (James 2:2).

That this should be the case is hardly surprising: the synagogue, as the regular place of worship, was an established place of weekly worship throughout the Greek speaking world – due the influence and needs of the widespread Jewish Diaspora – while the Temple was a central place of occasional worship. Now, it is a plain fact that no musical instruments were used in the worship of the synagogue – indeed, this remained the case until 1810 in Germany and remains the case in more orthodox synagogues to this day.

Undoubtedly, instruments were present in the corporate and formal temple ritual of sacrifice and festival – but their presence and use there, as we shall see, is explicitly regulated by God and is inextricably bound up with the Levites and with their offering of sacrifice.

Ordinary and Extraordinary Worship

All this serves to highlight an important distinction which needs to be borne in mind: that which exists between the *ordinary* and *extraordinary* public worship of God under the old covenant.

✦ The Synagogue

The *ordinary* and regular place of worship for the people of God under the old covenant was not the tabernacle, or the temple, but the synagogue – or the 'meeting place'. These meeting places (synagogues) were local places of worship and the people met to worship in them every Sabbath and, indeed, throughout the week for prayer and further teaching.

The increasing modern trend to view the synagogue as a kind of community centre rather than a place of worship is too revisionist by far and relies on slender evidence gathered so long after Biblical times as to be irrelevant. Clearly, meetings in the synagogue, on the Sabbath, were worship meetings. There were, indeed, other meetings for teaching and discipline, but it was essentially a place of worship or a 'house of prayer' (interruptions when our Lord preached – and indeed when Paul preached – were not representative of ordinary custom: they were due simply to the impression that gross heresy was being preached by those entrusted with expounding the law).

Presbyterianism has always appealed to the moral, simple and regular worship of the synagogue – diffused by the providence of God all over the world prior to the coming of the Messiah – as being not just a stark contrast to the ceremonial, complex and occasional worship of the temple but the single most effective means for the spread of the gospel when it arrived and the ready-made mould into which the new wine of the gospel would be poured.

This institution had office-bearers and a form of worship recognisable to Presbyterians and *contained no musical instruments in its worship and, significantly, Paul never debates their use in any of the synagogues he visits!*

+   The Temple

The *extraordinary* and occasional place of worship under the old covenant was the temple – a central building, located in Jerusalem, at which worship was indeed constantly being offered but, crucially, at which attendance was only required *three times a year*.

The reason for this distinction lay primarily in the fact that the temple was a standing figurative type of Christ and his work. Unsurprisingly, therefore, the temple contained much in the way of temporary types and symbols. It contained a priesthood, incense, altars, sacrifices, robes, holy bread, an Ark, sacred curtains, holy oil, holy incense – and much else. The synagogue, however, was simply an ordinary place of worship and contained a pulpit, benches for sitting on and a chest containing a copy of the scriptures – and its worship service consisted of prayers, praise reading and exposition.

Now, it is of tremendous significance that the temple contained the *musical accompaniment to the sacrifice* but that the worship of the weekly meeting place had *no instrumental music at all*! In other words, on the face of it, the case appears to be that the musical accompaniment, like the sacrifice it accompanied, was *temporary*, *typical* and *ceremonial*. We will attempt to demonstrate

> "Note the significance of their absence both from New Testament worship and *from the services of the whole of worshipping Christendom for the best part of the first 800 years of its existence"*

this in what follows below.

We will begin, then, by examining the precise role of musical instruments in the tabernacle and in the temple. Then, bearing in mind their absence from the weekly worship of the people of God in the synagogue, we will note the significance of their absence both from New Testament worship and *from the services of the whole of worshipping Christendom for the best part of the first 800 years of its existence.* Yes, you read that right: *their absence from the services of the whole of worshipping Christendom for the best part of the first 800 years of its existence!*

First, then, we will consider their use in the tabernacle and the temple.

Who authorises the use of instruments?

Although we associate Moses with the worship of the tabernacle onwards and associate David with the worship of the temple onwards – right down to the time of Christ – it is crucial to note that neither of them appointed any aspect of worship, including the use of musical instruments, without the *express command of God.*

Moses

We can begin with Moses, the public worship of God's people

and the tabernacle. It is fairly well known that Moses followed a pattern revealed to him by God when he appointed the worship of the tabernacle (Exodus 25:40). In spite of being 'learned in all the wisdom of the Egyptians' (Acts 7:20) – and doubtless being familiar with the wide array of musical instruments in use in Egypt in the realms of both the secular and the sacred – Moses commanded that the only musical instrument to be used in the public worship of the Tabernacle would be the trumpet. Its use is commanded in Numbers 10 and comes clearly from God. Note that its use was to be confined to the priesthood and to the appointed feasts. This worship prevailed for several hundred years.

David

In David's time, a major development takes place when the worship of God was centralised in Jerusalem. At this point, David appoints some of the Levites, under the oversight of Asaph, as professional singers and musicians ministering before the ark of the LORD in order to praise him – their role in carrying the tabernacle and its utensils had come to an end with the new central place of worship (1 Chronicles 23: 25, 26). Asaph himself was to sound the cymbals; Zechariah, Jeiel, Shemiramoth, Jehiel, Mattithiah, Eliab, Benaiah, Obed-edom, and Jeiel were to play harps and lyres and Benaiah and Jahaziel the priests were to blow the trumpets (1 Chronicles 16: 4-6).

Significantly, David made these appointments in obedience to *a specific command from God*. He makes this plain in his words to Solomon: in 1 Chronicles 28:19, David says that the changes he introduced were because 'The Lord made me understand all this in writing by his hand upon me – all the details of these plans' (1 Chronicles 28:19).

Moses and David normative for the Old Covenant

Nearly 200 years later, in a brief period of reform, Jehoiada restores the offerings under the control of the Levitical priests – 'with rejoicing and singing according *as it was established by David*' (1

Chronicles 23:18).

Moving on nearly 100 years further, when Hezekiah was reforming the nation – notably, beginning with the temple and its worship – he took care to carry out his reformation in accordance with the word of God. This meant that he only used the instruments that David had commanded to be used – which are referred to as 'God's instruments' (1 Chronicles 16:42). It is worth citing the passage in some detail: 'And he stationed the Levites in the house of the LORD with cymbals, with stringed instruments and with harps, *according to the commandment of David, of Gad the King's seer and of Nathan the prophet: for so was the commandment of the LORD through his prophets.* The Levites stood with the instruments of David, and the priests with the trumpets' (2 Chronicles 29:25-26).

It is important to note the authority source: God commands Gad and Nathan (the prophets) who, in turn, command David so that the Divine prophetic command comes to be recorded as normative in the scriptures. Accordingly, this God-given form of worship is adopted by Solomon in the temple (2 Chronicles 8:14) and this scripture later becomes the authority for Hezekiah in his reforms. He does not innovate on the issue of worship – even on the issue of musical instruments: he obeys.

Around 80 years later, during Josiah's Reformation, the King commands the Levites to organise themselves according to the commandments of David as they were found in scripture: 'And the singers, the sons of Asaph, were in their places *according to the command of David, Asaph, Heman and Jeduthun the King's seer'* (2 Chronicles 35:15).

Again, over half a millennium after David, following the return from the exile and with the rebuilding of the temple, we read that: 'When the builders laid the foundation of the temple of the Lord the priests stood in their apparel with trumpets and the Levites, the sons of Asaph, with cymbals, to praise the Lord, *according to the ordinance of David, King of Israel'* (Ezra 3:10).

Finally, around fifty years later, Nehemiah organises the

worship of the temple ensuring that the praise is '*with the musical instruments of David the man of God*' (Nehemiah 12:35, 36).

Daniel informs us (Daniel 3: 5-7) of a vast array of instruments being used in the culture and worship of Babylon but it is plain from what we have seen that exposure to the culture and worship of Babylon was no more influential on Ezra and Nehemiah than the culture and worship of Egypt was on Moses.

Where did the instruments come from?

Although it may surprise some, there is abundant evidence that the musical instruments used in the worship of God under the Old Covenant were designed and made exclusively for that purpose. In a sense, this ought to be no surprise. After all, the altars were unlike the Egyptian ones as were all the other items of furniture different from their Egyptian counterparts, so it should come as no real surprise to find that the instruments themselves were according to a special revelation from God to David. Consider the following.

First, the trumpet for use in the Tabernacle was of specific divine design (Numbers 10:1). This straight and narrow design was unlike the common curved design of most if not all other trumpets.

Second, the '*instruments of David*' (Nehemiah 12: 35-36) appear to be a reference to instruments which David designed and made rather than ones which he simply authorised or used.

After all, Amos refers to David as having 'invented' his instruments (Amos 6:5). The Hebrew used for 'inventing' is a reference to the creation of something new and is used of those who invented new weapons of warfare in the days of King Uzziah (2 Chronicles 26:15).

Furthermore, David specifically refers to the instruments being used in worship as 'musical instruments *which I made*...for giving praise' (1 Chronicles 23: 4-5). Again, the Hebrew word translated 'made' is used of forming an object – either creatively or according to a plan.

Therefore, the 'instruments of David' were ones which were devised, constructed and appointed by David according to the command of God.

Here, it is worthwhile noting again what we saw in connection with Hezekiah's reformation. We noted how he began with the reformation of the temple and its worship. On the issue of praise, he regulates the materials of praise and the musical accompaniment. As to the materials, Hezekiah fell back upon the inspired psalms of David and Asaph though the most recent of them were nearly 300 years old. As to musical accompaniment, again, Hezekiah does not innovate – he simply obeys. Consequently, we read that 'when the burnt offering began, the song of the Lord also began with the trumpets and the instruments of David king of Israel' (2 Chronicles 29:27).

Who was to play them?
It should have already become clear from our study that the instruments were to be played by the Levites. They were set apart to play. This is plain from 1 Chronicles 16: 4; 23: 1-5; 2 Chronicles 29: 25-26; 35: 3-10; Ezra 3:10 and Nehemiah 12:27.

It is also evident from the circumstances surrounding the Ark's return to Jerusalem. When David first tried to return the Ark, the judgement of God broke out against him, against Uzzah – who was chastised by death for touching the Ark – and indeed against all Israel. This judgment came because the commands of God were not closely followed regarding the Ark (1 Chronicles 15:13). Note that on this occasion, 'David and all Israel played music before God with all their might, with singing, on harps, on stringed instruments, on tambourines, on cymbals and with trumpets' (1 Chronicles 13:8).

However, after humbling and chastisement, David successfully returns the Ark to Jerusalem. Note that on this occasion, the instruments are played by the Levites alone (1 Chronicles 15: 14-24). *Clearly, careless disregard for the use of musical instruments was part of the reason for the chastisement of God upon David and the church!*

Why, then, were the musical instruments only to be played by the Levites? The answer to this lies in reason for their use – specifically, in the occasions on which they were to be played.

When were they to be played?

Careful study of the scriptures reveals that, in acts of worship, musical instruments were to be played by the Levites *as an accompaniment to the sacrificial ritual in the temple.* In 2 Chronicles 29:27-28, we read:

> *'And when the burnt offering began, the song of the Lord also began, with the trumpets and with the instruments of David king of Israel. So all the assembly worshipped, the singers sang, and the trumpeters sounded; all this continued until the burnt offering was finished'.*

What was their function?

If we consider all the above carefully – the appointment of the instruments, who made them, who played them and when and where they were to be played – it is hard to avoid the conclusion that their role in worship was *symbolic* and *ceremonial.*

This ought to be no surprise. In this respect, their presence was no different from other symbolic accompaniments to the tabernacle/temple ritual and their use little different from the incense accompanying the prayers. If the incense accompanying the prayer spoke of the sweetness of the prayers before God, then it would seem fairly clear that the musical accompaniment along with the sacrifice spoke of something too: most likely, the spiritual joy in the heart of the believer.

Aside from the few references to musical instruments being used in national celebration, as well as on social occasions (as in, for example, Judges 31:24 and 1 Samuel 18:6), the picture brought before us is one where musical accompaniment, like the sacrifice which it accompanies, is tightly regulated by God.

The Silence of the New Testament

As to the silence in the New Testament regarding music, the writer of the paper referred to above offers the following missiological reason:

> '... I want to highlight the missiological significance of that silence. The Gospel was to go into every culture in the world, into every musical culture in the world, to be translated into each. There was no command to go into music-making cultures and forbid them to use their traditional instruments. There was no command to go into Gentile cultures and insist they use Jewish instruments. There was simply nothing new said about the matter. The Old Testament had said enough to make the permission clear. The aim now was to take the Gospel to all, so that more and more might praise the Lord and move the world towards the fulfilment of the vision seen in Psalm 150.'

Two observations need to be made here.

First, although the writer speaks of *permission* to praise with instruments, it is clearly more than that. If the Old Testament commands are our warrant, it contains *commands* as opposed to bare permission. Is there not, in the Psalms, a *command* to use them? Is this command still valid? If so, why are we at liberty to disobey it? Clearly, a proper application of the Old Testament command would make their use compulsory rather than optional.

Second, although the 'missiological theory' sounds quite interesting, it also sounds far too much like an after-the-fact rationalisation and special pleading in the critical absence of evidence. In the midst of a plethora of references to worship in the New Testament, a more satisfactory explanation than this for the silence regarding the use of musical instruments is surely required.

Can we provide one? Yes.

We have already noted the absence of musical instruments from the ordinary, weekly public worship of God's people in the synagogue right up to the days of the Christ and the Apostles.

Also, it is the case that while the core elements of ordinary synagogue worship appear in the practice of the New Testament churches, none of the ceremonial parts of temple worship appear there. As said already, it is the mode of synagogue worship which was adopted by the New Testament church. And it is easy to see why. All that was required to transform the synagogue from the ordinary weekly place of Jewish worship on the old Sabbath to the ordinary place of weekly Christian worship on the Lord's Day (or Christian Sabbath) was simply the recognition that the Messiah being preached had come! This would require simply adding the New Testament books to the canon as they were written and admitting into the worship the new covenant sacraments. The rest remains the same: the psalms – with no instrumental accompaniment – prayers, readings and proclamation. We find abundant reference to all these in the New Testament churches – but none to instruments, altars, candles, vestments or incense.

However, it is not the case that we need to argue from silence alone. Some of the references to singing in the New Testament indicate that this singing was indeed unaccompanied.

In Ephesians 5:19, we are commanded to be 'making melody to the Lord with all (our) heart'. More literally we are being asked to '*pluck the strings* of our heart'. It is not hard to see an intended contrast here between what is to be plucked in the simple and more spiritual worship of the new covenant – the heart – and what is to be plucked in the more earthly, and ceremonial worship of the old covenant – the stringed instrument. Similarly, in an epistle which

"Similarly, in an epistle which constantly contrasts the old with the new, our 'sacrifice of praise' consists of the 'fruit of our lips' (Hebrews 13:15)"

constantly contrasts the old with the new, our 'sacrifice of praise' consists of the 'fruit of our lips' (Hebrews 13:15).

What is even more remarkable is the witness of the early church from the days of the Apostles onwards.

The witness of the early church

Although this paper is concerned primarily with Biblical teaching, there is a particularly strong reason why a reference to the practice of the early church, and especially to the era immediately following that of the Apostles, is important in this case.

As to the facts, it is beyond question that the early Church Fathers were opposed to the use of musical instruments in Christian worship. What is most remarkable about this opposition, however, is how *uniform* and how *vehement* it is. The Fathers are, on this issue, absolutely unanimous!

Sometimes, admittedly, their opposition was on the weaker ground that such instruments were so deeply associated with pagan and immoral practices. However, they also plainly believed that their use belonged to the church in her infancy – when she was being trained by types and ceremonies under the old covenant – not in her attainment of adulthood under the new covenant.

The reason why such a universal testimony is important lies in this: if it was indeed the case that worship with musical accompaniment was the Apostolic practice in all the churches of the New Testament in Europe and Asia and the Middle East, *it simply becomes impossible to believe that no church Father, in the era following the Apostles, is prepared to defend their use!*

If the evidence from the Fathers was not uniform – as is the case on some other issues – this would cease to be such a difficulty but this uniformity of witness among all the Church Fathers (some of whom virtually overlap with the Apostles) and reaching down into the 8th century is *simply irreconcilable* with the theory that the Apostles ordained and established churches which used the accompaniment of musical instruments with their sung praise.

For the sake of completion, it may be useful to complete the historical survey. The absence of musical accompaniment prevailed, universally, until the eighth century when the first organ was introduced into the worship of the Western Church. Even from then, in the West, their use was rare and, as late as the 13th century, this continued to be the case. From the 14th century, their use became increasingly common. The Eastern Church refrained from using them – and continues to do so today.

Returning to the West, the Reformation Churches – in distinction, here, from the Lutheran church – abolished their use. Both Zwingli (an accomplished musician) and Calvin were strongly opposed to it. The exception often cited - that of the Dutch Church - hardly constitutes a valid exception in that the Pastors were opposed to their use on the ground that it was unbiblical. The decision to allow instrumental pieces before and after the worship was merely a concession to the power of the civil authorities. Even then, the organ was originally not used to accompany the singing of Psalms.

Surprisingly, perhaps, the Anglican Church, in its early literature, made plain its desire to be without musical instruments in worship – see, for example, the 'Homily on the Place and Time of Prayer' in the 'Second Book of Homilies' (1563).

In Scotland, the ban was total following the Reformation

and this situation remained unchanged until the 19th century when four successive decades witnessed the introduction of musical instruments into Scottish public worship: The Congregationalists were first in the 1850s, followed by the Church of Scotland in 1860s, the United Presbyterians in the 1870s and the Free Church of Scotland in 1880s – the use of hymns had already been permitted by the Free Church in 1872.

Most Reformed churches have admitted hymns and music into their worship from around the same period as those in Scotland and use them with increasing freedom in contemporary worship – increasingly so with the birth and rapid growth of the Pentecostal and Charismatic movements.

Does the church have liberty to introduce musical instruments?
Since the worship of the Temple has expired along with its priesthood, the only way in which their introduction would be justified would be by an explicit directive from Christ or the Apostles authorising their use. In other words, having expired with the temple and the Levitical priesthood, the inspiration of the Spirit of God is as necessary for introducing musical instrumentation into our covenantal offering to God as it is for the introduction of new song.

Of course, most advocates for their use would argue that the nature of the instruments and their use under the New Covenant must be left to the same on-going guidance of the Spirit in the new covenant church as the provision of songs to be sung. However, this raises an interesting problem: at the human level, whose guidance do we accept for both? If the use of the instruments and, as we have seen in Chapter I, the content of the song, is a matter of *prophetic revelation*, then, as Reformed Christians, we must be content to let the Bible have the final word. Without such clear prophetic guidance from the Holy Spirit, we are left with what we have experienced over the last 150 years, relying on men supposedly 'guided' by the Spirit: the ever-increasing liturgical chaos now prevalent in Western Christendom.

The only way to arrest this decline would be through the imposition of rules and regulations by human authority. These rules would, themselves, be extremely offensive to any number of people who would desire something else. Interestingly, the strengthened concept of authority prevents the older orthodox communions from the same problem – and they remain non-instrumental and heavily dominated by psalmody.

In churches which adhere to other forms of government, what you have, of necessity, by introducing musical instruments into the worship of God, is the opening of Pandora's Box out of which everything and anything can come – and absolutely nothing can be done about it.

Who, after all, is to decide how the musical aspect of the worship of God should be conducted? Advocates of musical instruments must recognize that David had specific Divine instructions for the *identity, introduction and use* of these instruments. This has invariably led to the creation of 'worship committees' and the questions they invariably need to deal with: How many instruments are to be used? Is it to be a band or an orchestra? Are the instruments merely to accompany or are they to perform a music ministry on their own? As Erasmus said in the 16th century, 'We have brought a cumbersome and theatrical music into our churches...the church rings with the noise of trumpets, pipes and dulcimers and human voices strive to bear their part with them. Men run to church as to a theatre, to have their ears tickled.'

These issues are of increasing importance in an age when the simplicity of singing congregational hymns to an upright piano, or organ, has given way to hugely differing styles of music ministry. Some, while arguing for the use of instruments, try to retain some kind of control by also arguing for simplicity or economy of use under the new covenant. But why should this be? If our authority for musical accompaniment arises from Psalms such as Psalm 150, such pleas for simplicity can only sound rather hollow – or indeed, blasphemous. After all, if we are commanded to use many instruments, why are we now to follow 'simplicity'? If a stringed instrument is commanded, why have we liberty to do without it?

Most advocates of musical accompaniment recognise this and dispense with the simplicity argument altogether. However, the new 'freedom' has its own obvious pitfalls. Undeniably, the increased use of music and its increasingly varied forms has led to alienation and division. Many churches are now being increasingly divided by these music styles – sometimes according to age and taste. In one way, this is no surprise: when the simplicity and universality of the Apostolic rule and practice is set aside, complexity and division inevitably follow. *In worship, as in doctrine, when you add (to God's commandments) you divide (God's people)!*

Note that this is not an argument based on the practical difficulty of deciding what to sing and how it is to be accompanied. These practical issues are, of course, real and important – but it is worth noting that the reason praise under the old covenant was not encumbered with the same practical problems as are experienced today was because, at least in connection with the public worship, the use of music *was tightly regulated by prophetic authority*: the number of instruments, their kind, their precise use – when and how – all this was explicitly stipulated by David in response to the express command of God!

Finally, it is worth noting two other things.

A ban on the use of musical instruments in public worship does not invalidate their use generally – music and musical instruments are clearly gifts of God. In fact, such a ban on instruments does not even invalidate their use in the more general sense of giving praise to God rather than in the more specific offering of worship.

Again, and on a practical note, it is not necessary to hold the position that the use of instrumental music in public worship necessarily invalidates the *whole service* of worship. When all is said and done, it is not our business to say exactly what God accepts or rejects but only what he requires and expects. Such questions arise for everyone: for example, does a non-Presbyterian think that the ministry of a Ruling Elder is completely invalid because he considers his 'office' to be without Biblical foundation? Does a Presbyterian believe that a Bishop has no valid ministry just because his office is without Biblical warrant – Bishop Ryle, for example? Does a Baptist accept the sprinkled baptism of an adult Presbyterian? In other words, it is hardly

> "On a practical note, it is not necessary to hold the position that the use of instrumental music in public worship necessarily invalidates the *whole service* of worship"

reasonable to suggest that only those who believe in exclusive Psalm singing need to confront issues of this kind. In this way, it is possible, on some occasions, to conceive of God accepting the worship offered while still disapproving of the use of the musical instruments, while on other occasions, rejecting it.

However, as I indicated above, whether or not God accepts or rejects particular acts of worship – or indeed the worshipper – is not the business of the church. Neither is it an issue to play around with and take chances on. Who would have thought that God's chastising anger would break out against Uzzah simply for trying to steady the ark of God? Undoubtedly, it has much to do with the *degree of knowledge* involved on the part of the worshipper and, indeed, on whether the worshipper is *turning away from the truth* or *moving towards it*. God does not deal as graciously with a people departing from a biblical position as he does with a people groping towards one. While it is undoubtedly the case that many churches have been blessed while using hymns and instruments – it is not so evident that any church has been blessed by taking the decision to abandon unaccompanied psalm singing. All this is a solemn reminder that while everything matters to God, he alone discerns the heart. For us, in Scotland, we could well do with remembering that all our actions are the actions of churches spawned from the Second Reformation and in a covenanted land.

So, it is our duty to follow the Truth where it leads – not blindly to follow others or to speculate as to what God will do. Judgment is God's business – not ours. It is the duty of those who believe this form of worship to be the correct one, and the duty of the confessing church, to articulate this truth and to *follow, defend* and *promote* it.

CONCLUSION

It is our conclusion, then, that the Book of Psalms was compiled for the use of the church in singing praise to God and that the church is not at liberty to add to this book, to supplement it or to replace it.

It is also our conclusion that the facts surrounding the silence of the New Testament on the issue of musical instruments, properly understood, constitute a compelling case for interpreting that silence as evidence that no instrumental music was used in the worship of the New Testament church.

It is also our desire that the Lord would strengthen us to restore the practice of unaccompanied psalm singing as part of that true reformation and true spiritual revival for which we long and for which we need, more earnestly, to pray.

Rev. Kenneth Stewart is the minister of the Glasgow congregation of the Reformed Presbyterian Church of Scotland.

Appendix

Minority Report
of The Committee on Song in the Public Worship of God Submitted to the Fourteenth General Assembly of the Orthodox Presbyterian Church

John Murray & William Young

INTRODUCTION

The above-mentioned committee presented to the Thirteenth General Assembly a report bearing upon the question of the regulative principle of worship. This principle is to the effect that divine warrant or authorization is required for every element entering into the worship of God. In the words of the Confession of Faith of this Church, 'The acceptable way of worshipping the true God is instituted by Himself, and so limited by His own revealed will that He may not be worshipped according to the imaginations and devices of men, or the suggestions of Satan, under any visible representation, or any other way not prescribed in the holy Scripture' (Chapt. XXI, Sect. I).

In terms of the commission given by the Eleventh General Assembly and in accordance with the regulative principle set forth in the report of the committee, presented to the Thirteenth General Assembly, the question with which this report is concerned is:

What does the Scripture warrant or prescribe respecting the songs that may be sung in the public worship of God?

In dealing with this question it should be appreciated that the singing of God's praise is a distinct act of worship. It is to be distinguished, for example, from the reading of the Scripture and from the offering of prayer to God. It is, of course, true that songs of praise often include what is of the nature of prayer to God, as it is also true that in the offering of prayer to God there is much that is of the nature of praise and thanksgiving. But it is not proper to appeal to the divine authorization or warrant we possess as to the content of prayer in order to determine the question as to the content of song. Prayer is one element of worship, singing is another. Similarity or even identity of content does not in the least obliterate the distinction between these two specific kinds of exercise in the worship of God. Because of this distinction we may not say that the offering of prayer and the singing of praise to God are the same thing and argue from the divine authorization we possess respecting the one to the authorization respecting the other. One or two examples may be given of the necessity and importance of guarding the distinctiveness of the several parts of worship and of determining from the Scripture what its prescriptions are respecting each element.

Both reports submitted by this committee are agreed that some Scripture songs may be sung in the public worship of God. But these Scripture songs may also be read as Scripture and they may be used in preaching. In such cases the actual materials are the same. But reading the Scripture is not the same exercise of worship as singing, and neither is preaching the same as singing, or reading the Scripture. The same kind of distinction applies to the exercises of praying and singing even when the content is identical.

The Lord's Supper is an act of thanksgiving as well as one of commemoration and communion. But though the partaking of the bread and the wine includes thanksgiving, just as prayer and singing do, yet the celebration of the Lord's Supper is an act of worship distinct from both prayer and singing, and the divine prescriptions respecting the celebration of the Lord's Supper cannot be determined by the divine prescriptions regarding prayer or singing but must rather be derived from the revelation God has given respecting the observance of that distinct element of the worship of God.

Consequently the minority contends that the argument used in the report of the committee, to wit, that, since we are not limited in our prayers to the words of Scripture or to the 'prayers' given us in Scripture, therefore the same freedom is granted in song, is invalid. We may not argue thus from the divine warrant respecting one element to the divine warrant respecting another. The question of the divine prescription regarding the songs that may be sung in the public worship of God must be answered, therefore, on the basis of the teaching of Scripture with respect to that specific element of worship.

When we address ourselves to the question of the teaching of Scripture we find that the New Testament does not provide us with copious instruction on this matter. It is for that reason that we are placed under the necessity of exercising great care lest we overstep the limits of divine authorization and warrant. This report will deal with the evidence that is directly germane to the question.

THE SCRIPTURE EVIDENCE
I. Matthew 26:30; Mark 14:26.
Here we are told that, on the occasion of the passover, Jesus and His disciples sang a hymn before going out to the Mount of Olives. The Greek is *humnesantes*, which literally means 'having hymned'. The evidence available to us from other sources is to the effect of indicating that the hymn sung on this occasion was what is known as the Hallel, consisting of Psalms 113-118. This instance evinces the following facts.

(1) No warrant whatsoever can be adduced for the singing of uninspired hymns. There is no evidence that an uninspired

hymn was sung on this occasion.

(2) The evidence we do possess evinces that Jesus and His disciples sang a portion of the psalter.

(3) The singing took place in connection with the celebration of the Old Testament sacrament of the Passover and the New Testament sacrament of the Lord's Supper.

II. 1 Corinthians 14:15, 26.

Paul is here dealing with the assembly of the saints for worship. He says, 'I will sing with the spirit and I will sing with the understanding also' (vs. 15), 'Each one hath a psalm' (vs. 26). From the verb that Paul uses in verse 15 we might quite properly translate as follows: 'I will sing a psalm with the spirit and I will sing a psalm with the understanding also,' just as in verse 26 he says, 'Each one hath a psalm.' We must conclude, therefore, that psalms were sung in the church at Corinth and such singing has, by obvious implication, the apostle's sanction and is confirmed by his example.

The question does arise: What were these psalms? It is possible that they were charismatic psalms. If so, one thing is certain—they were not uninspired compositions. If charismatic they were inspired or given by the Holy Spirit. If we today possessed such charismatic psalms, sung by the apostle himself in the assemblies of worship or sanctioned by him in the worship of the church, then we should have the proper authority for the use of them in the songs of the sanctuary. It so happens, however, that we do not have conclusive evidence to show that we have any of such alleged charismatic psalms. But even on the hypothesis that they were charismatic psalms and even on the hypothesis that we have examples of such in Acts 4:23-30; 1 Timothy 3:16, we are not thereby furnished with any authorization for the use of uninspired songs in the worship of God.

On the hypothesis that they were not charismatic psalms we have to ask, what were they? To answer this question we have simply to ask another: what songs in the usage of Scripture, fall into the category of psalms? There is one answer. The Book of

Psalms is composed of psalms and, therefore, by the simplest principle of hermeneutics we can say that, in terms of Scripture language, the songs that are repeatedly called psalms perfectly satisfy the denotation and connotation of the word 'psalm' as it is used here. If inspired Scripture says, 'Each one hath a psalm', and Scripture also calls the 'Psalms' psalms, then surely we may also sing a Psalm to the praise of God in His worship.

So far as these two texts are concerned we can say that they provide us with no warrant whatsoever for the use of uninspired hymns. We can also say that, since the psalms we possess in the psalter are certainly psalms in the terminology of Scripture itself, we are hereby provided with divine warrant for the singing of such in the worship of God.

III. Ephesians 5:19; Colossians 3:16

With respect to these two texts it should be noted, first of all, that Paul is not necessarily referring to the public worship of God. The context does not make clear that Paul is confining himself here to exhortation that concerns the behaviour of believers in relation to one another in the assemblies of worship. Paul may very well be giving general exhortation. Indeed, the context in both passages would appear to show that he is exhorting to a certain kind of exercise in which believers should engage in reference to one another in the discharge of that mutual instruction and edification requisite to concerted advancement of one another's highest interests and of the glory of God.

This consideration does not, however, remove these texts from relevancy to the question of the public worship of God. For, if Paul specifies psalms, hymns and Spiritual songs as the media through which believers may mutually promote the glory of God and one another's edification in those more generic Christian exercises, this fact has very close bearing upon the question of the apostolically sanctioned and authorized media of praise to God in the more specific worship of the sanctuary. In other words, if the apostolically enjoined media or materials of song in the more generic exercises of worship are psalms, hymns and Spiritual songs, then surely nothing inferior to psalms, hymns and Spiritual songs would be enjoined for use in the more specific exercises of worship in the assemblies of the church. If psalms, hymns and Spiritual songs are the limits of the materials of song in praise of God in less formal acts of worship, how much more are they the limits in more formal acts of worship. With respect to these two texts the following considerations are to be borne in mind.

(1) We cannot determine the denotation or connotation of psalms, hymns and Spiritual songs by any modern usage of these same words. The meaning and reference must be determined by the usage of Scripture.

(2) Some of the facts with reference to the usage of Scripture are very significant.

The word *psalmos* (psalm) occurs some 94 times in the Greek Scriptures, that is to say, some 87 times in the Septuagint version of the Old Testament and 7 times in the New Testament. In the Septuagint some 78 of these instances are in the Book of Psalms. In the great majority of instances in the Book of Psalms, some 67 in all, it occurs in the titles of the Psalms. In three of the seven instances in the New Testament the word is unmistakably used with reference to the Psalms, in two instances in the phrase the 'Book of Psalms' (*biblos psalmon*) and in the other instance with reference to the second Psalm. It is surely significant, therefore, that in some 70 of the 94 instances the reference is clearly to the Book of Psalms or to Psalms in the Book of Psalms.

The word *humnos* (hymn) occurs some 19 times in the Greek Bible, 17 times in the Old Testament and 2 times in the New (in the passages under consideration). Of the 17 Old Testament instances 13 occur in the Book of Psalms and 6 of these are in the titles. In the seven instances not occurring in the titles the reference is in each case to the praise of God, or to the songs of Sion. The other four instances in the other books of the Old Testament have likewise reference to the songs of praise to God.

The word, *odee* (song) occurs some 86 times in the Greek

Bible, some 80 times in the Old Testament and 6 times in the New. Apart from these two passages (Ephesians 5:19; Colossians 3:16), it occurs in the New Testament only in the Book of Revelation. Of the 80 occurrences in the Old Testament some 45 are in the Book of Psalms and 36 of these are in the titles of the Psalms.

It is surely apparent, therefore, how large a proportion of the occurrences of these words is in the Book of Psalms. These facts of themselves do not prove that the reference here in Ephesians 5:19; Colossians 3:16 is to the Book of Psalms exclusively. But these facts must not be forgotten as we proceed to determine the character of the lyrical compositions mentioned in these two texts.

(3) In the New Testament the word *psalmos* occurs seven times, as was just stated. Two of these instances are in the texts we are considering. One of these instances is 1 Corinthians 14:26, a text dealt with already. Two instances (Luke 20:42; Acts 1:20) refer to the Book of Psalms (*biblos psalmon*). Luke 24:44 clearly refers to Old Testament inspired Scripture and probably to the Book of Psalms. Acts 13:33 refers to the second Psalm. In none of these instances is there any warrant for supposing that 'psalms' refer to uninspired human compositions. In the majority, without the least shadow of doubt, the reference is to inspired Scripture.

In the New Testament the word *humnos* occurs only in these two passages. The verb *humneo* (to hymn) occurs four times (Matthew 26:30; Mark 14:26, Acts 16:25; Hebrews 2:12). As we found already, the synoptic passages most probably refer to the singing of the Hallel by our Lord and His disciples. Acts 16:25 refers to the singing of Paul and Silas in prison. Hebrews 2:12 is a quotation from the Old Testament (Psalm 22:23)—*en meso ekklesias humneso se.*

No evidence whatsoever can be adduced from the usage in support of the use of uninspired hymns.

Apart from these two instances the word *odee* occurs in the New Testament only in Revelation 5:9; 14:3 (2); 15:3.

From the New Testament, then, no evidence can be

derived to show that these words may be used here (Ephesians 5:19; Colossians 3:16) with reference to uninspired songs. Even though *odee* is used in the Book of Revelation with reference to songs other than those in the Book of Psalms it is not used there with reference to uninspired human compositions but with reference to inspired songs.

(4) We now come to the consideration of some facts which are even more significant than those already discussed. The Book of Psalms is composed of psalms, hymns and songs. We have already found that the overwhelming majority of the instances of these words in both Testaments has reference to the Book of Psalms. We now come to the discussion of the meaning of these words in the titles of the Psalms.

In the Septuagint *psalmos* occurs some 67 times in the titles to the Psalms. In most cases it is the translation of the Hebrew *mismor*, but in a few cases it translates other Hebrew words. *Psalmos* means simply 'song of praise.' The frequency with which the word *psalmos* occurs in the titles is probably the reason why the Book of Psalms is called in the LXX version simply *psalmoi*. In the Hebrew it is called *tehillim*.

It is perfectly obvious, therefore, that the New Testament writers, familiar as they were with the Old Testament in Greek, would necessarily have the Book of Psalms in mind when they used this word *psalmos*. There is no other piece of evidence that even begins to take on the significance for the meaning of the word 'psalm' in the New Testament that this simple fact takes on, namely, that the Book of Psalms was called simply 'Psalms' (*psalmoi*). The usage of the New Testament itself puts this beyond all doubt. There the Psalms are called the Book of Psalms.

There is nothing in the context of these two passages requiring us to regard 'psalms' as referring to uninspired compositions. On the other hand, there are abundant instances in the usage of Scripture elsewhere which show that the word 'psalm' refers to an inspired composition. Furthermore, there is no instance in which the word 'psalm,' as used with reference to a song of praise to God, can be shown to refer to an uninspired song. It is therefore quite unwarranted to regard 'psalms' in these two passages as referring to uninspired songs, whereas there is abundant warrant for regarding them as denoting inspired compositions. Consequently, if we are to follow the line of the evidence provided by the Scripture, we are forced to find the 'psalms' here mentioned within the limits of inspiration.

As we found, the word *humnos* appears some 17 times in the Septuagint version. In thirteen cases it appears in the Book of Psalms. In five or six cases it appears in the titles of the Psalms as the translation of the Hebrew *neginoth* or *neginah*. It is significant that on several occasions in the text of the Psalms *humnos* translates the Hebrew word *tehillah*, which is the word used to designate the Book of Psalms in the Hebrew. This shows that psalms may be called hymns and hymns are psalms. Psalms and hymns are not exclusive of one another. A psalm may be not only a psalm but also a hymn.

These facts show that when, in the usage of Scripture, we look for the type of composition meant by a 'hymn,' we find it in the Psalms. And we have no evidence whatsoever that a hymn, in the usage of Scripture, ever designates an uninspired human composition.

The word *odee* occurs much more frequently in the titles of the Psalms than does the word *humnos*, but not as frequently as does the word *psalmos*. There are some 36 instances. It usually translates the Hebrew word *shir* but not always. Occasionally it is the translation of *mismor*, the word generally translated by *psalmos*. *Odee* occurs so frequently in the titles of the psalms that its meaning would be definitely influenced by that usage.

The conclusion to which we are driven then is that the frequency with which these words occur in that book of the Old Testament that is unique in this respect that it is a collection of songs composed at various times and by various inspired writers, the book that stands out distinctively and uniquely as composed of psalms, hymns and songs, would tend most definitely to fix the meaning of these words in the usage of the inspired writers. The case is simply this that beyond all dispute there is no other datum that compares with the significance of the language of the Septuagint in the resolution of this question. When taken in conjunction with the only positive evidence we have in the New Testament, the evidence leads preponderantly to the conclusion that when Paul wrote 'psalms, hymns and Spiritual songs' he would expect the minds of his readers to think of what were, in the terms of Scripture itself, 'psalms, hymns and Spiritual songs,' namely, the Book of Psalms.

(5) The evidence does not warrant the conclusion that the apostle meant by 'psalms, hymns and Spiritual songs' to designate three distinct groups or types of lyrical compositions. It is significant in this connection that in a few cases in the titles of the Psalms all three of these words occur. In many cases the words 'psalm' and 'song' occur in the same title. This shows that a lyrical composition may be a psalm, hymn and song at the same time.

The words, of course, have their own distinctive meanings, and such distinctive meanings may intimate the variety and richness of the materials of song the apostle has in mind. Paul uses three words that in the established usage of Scripture designate the rich variety of such lyrical compositions as were suited for the worship of God in the service of song.

(6) Paul specifies the character of the songs as 'Spiritual'— *odais pneumatikais*. If anything should be obvious from the use of the word *pneumatikos* in the New Testament it is that it has reference to the Holy Spirit and means, in such contexts as the present, 'given by the Spirit.' Its meaning is not at all, as Trench contends, 'such as were composed by spiritual men, and moved in the sphere of spiritual things' (*Synonyms*, LXXVIII). It rather means, as Meyer points out, 'proceeding from the Holy Spirit, as *theopneustos*' (Commentary on Ephesians 5:19). In this context the word would mean 'indited by the Spirit,' just as in 1 Corinthians 2:13 *logois...pneumatikois* are 'words inspired by the Spirit' and 'taught by the Spirit' (*didaktois pneumatos*).

The question, of course, arises: why does the word *pneumatikos* qualify *odais* and not *psalmois* and *humnois*? A reasonable answer to this question is that *pneumatikais* qualifies all three datives and that its gender (feminine) is due to attraction to the gender of the noun that is closest to it. Another distinct possibility, made particularly plausible by the omission of the copulative in Colossians 3:16, is that 'Spiritual songs' are the genus of which 'psalms' and 'hymns' are the species. This is the view of Meyer, for example.

On either of these assumptions the psalms, hymns and songs are all 'Spiritual' and therefore all inspired by the Holy Spirit. The bearing of this upon the question at issue is perfectly apparent. Uninspired hymns are immediately excluded.

But we shall have to allow for the distinct possibility that the word 'Spiritual,' in the grammatical structure of the clause, is confined to the word 'songs.' On this hypothesis the 'songs' are characterized as 'Spiritual,' and therefore characterized as inspired or indited by the Holy Spirit. This, at least, should be abundantly clear.

The question would arise then: is it merely the 'songs' that need, to be inspired while the 'psalms' and 'hymns' may be uninspired? The asking of the question shows the unreasonableness of such an hypothesis, especially when we bear in mind all that has already been shown with reference to the use of these words. On what conceivable ground would Paul have insisted that the 'songs' needed to be divinely inspired while the 'psalms' and 'hymns' did not need to be? In the usage of Scripture there was no hard and fast line of distinction between psalms and hymns, on the one hand, and songs on the other. It would be quite impossible to find any good ground for such discrimination in the apostolic prescription.

The unreasonableness of such a supposition appears all the more conclusive when we remember the Scripture usage with respect to the word 'psalms.' There is not the least bit of evidence to suppose that in such usage on the part of the apostle 'psalm' could mean an uninspired human composition. All the evidence, rather, goes to establish the opposite conclusion.

We see then that psalms are inspired. Songs are inspired because they are characterized as 'Spiritual.' What then about the hymns? May they be uninspired? As already indicated, it would be an utterly unreasonable hypothesis to maintain that the apostle would require that songs be inspired while psalms and hymns might not. This becomes all the more cogent when we recognize, as we have established, that the psalms and songs were inspired. It would indeed be strange discrimination if hymns might be uninspired and psalms and songs inspired. But it would be strange to the point of absurdity if Paul should be supposed to insist that songs had to be inspired but hymns not. For what distinction can be drawn between a hymn and a song that would make it requisite for the latter to be inspired while the former might not be? We, indeed, cannot be sure that there is any distinction so far as actual denotation is concerned. Even if we do maintain the distinct colour of each word there is no discoverable reason why so radical a distinction as that between inspiration and non-inspiration could be maintained.

The only conclusion we can arrive at then is that 'hymns' in Ephesians 5:19, Colossians 3:16 must be accorded the same 'Spiritual' quality as is accorded to 'psalms' by obvious implication and to 'songs' by express qualification and that this was taken for granted by the apostle, either because the word 'Spiritual' would be regarded as qualifying all three words, or because 'Spiritual songs' were the genus of which 'psalms' and 'hymns' were the species, or because in the usage of the church 'hymns' like 'psalms' would be recognized in their own right and because of the context in which they are mentioned to be in no other category, as respects their 'Spiritual' quality, than the category occupied by psalms and songs.

In reference to these two passages, then, we are compelled to conclude:

(a) There is no warrant for thinking that 'psalms, hymns

and Spiritual songs' can refer to uninspired human compositions. These texts provide us with no authorization whatsoever for the singing of uninspired songs in the worship of God.

(b) There is warrant for concluding that 'psalms, hymns and Spiritual songs' refer to inspired compositions. These texts provide us, therefore, with warrant for the singing of inspired songs in the worship of God.

(c) The Book of Psalms provides us with psalms, hymns and songs that are inspired and therefore with the kind of compositions referred to in Ephesians 5:19, Colossians 3:16.

GENERAL CONCLUSIONS

This survey of the evidence derived from Scripture shows, in the judgment of the minority, that there is no evidence from Scripture that can be adduced to warrant the singing of uninspired human compositions in the public worship of God. The report of the committee maintains that we do have warrant for the use of such songs. The minority is well aware of the plausibility of the arguments of the committee, to wit, the argument drawn from the analogy of prayer and the argument drawn from the necessity of expanding the content of song to keep pace with the expansion of the revelation given in the New Testament. The former of these arguments has been dealt with in the earlier part of this report. The latter is much more cogent. T here are, however, two considerations that require to be mentioned by way of answer.

(i) We have no evidence either from the Old Testament or from the New that the expansion of revelation received expression in the devotional exercises of the church through the singing of uninspired songs of praise. This is a fact that cannot be discounted. If we possessed evidence that in the Old Testament period the church gave expression to revelation as it progressed by the singing of uninspired songs in the worship of God, then the argument from analogy would be rather conclusive, especially in view of the relative silence of the New Testament. But no evidence has been produced to prove the use of uninspired songs in the worship of the Old Testament. Or, if instances of the use of uninspired songs in the worship of the New Testament could be adduced, then the argument of the committee would be established. But the very cases adduced by the committee to show that there was an expansion of song in the New Testament do not show that uninspired songs were employed. Hence we are compelled to conclude that, since there is no evidence to show the use of uninspired songs in the practice of the church in the New Testament, the argument of the committee cannot plead authorization from the Scriptures. The church of God must in this matter, as in all other matters concerned with the actual content of worship, confine itself to the limits of Scripture authorization, and it is the contention of the minority that we do not possess evidence on the basis of which to plead the use of uninspired songs in the public worship of God.

The argument of the committee that 'the New Testament deals with conditions in the early church which have not been continued and which cannot be our present norm' fails to take due account of the normative character of Scripture. It is true that we today do not have the gift of inspiration and, therefore, we cannot compose inspired songs. But the Scripture does prescribe for us the way in which we are to worship God in the conditions that are permanent in the church. And since the Scripture does warrant and prescribe the use of inspired songs but does not warrant the use of uninspired songs, we are to restrict ourselves to those inspired materials made available to us by the Scripture itself. In other words, the Scripture does not provide us with any warrant for the exercising of those gifts the church now possesses in the composition of the actual content of song.

(ii) If the argument drawn from the expansion of revelation is applied within the limits of Scripture authorization, then the utmost that can be established is the use of New Testament songs or of New Testament materials adapted to singing. Principally the minority is not jealous to insist that New Testament songs may not be used in the worship of God. What we are most jealous to maintain is that Scripture does authorize the use of inspired songs, that is, Scripture songs, and that the singing of other than Scripture songs in the worship of God has no warrant from the Word of God and is therefore forbidden.

On the basis of these studies the minority respectfully submits to the Fourteenth General Assembly the following conclusions:

1. There is no warrant in Scripture for the use of uninspired human compositions in the singing of God's praise in public worship.

2. There is explicit authority for the use of inspired songs.

3. The songs of divine worship must therefore be limited to the songs of Scripture, for they alone are inspired.

4. The Book of Psalms does provide us with the kind of compositions for which we have the authority of Scripture.

5. We are therefore certain of divine sanction and approval in the singing of the Psalms.

6. We are not certain that other inspired songs were intended to be sung in the worship of God, even though the use of other inspired songs does not violate the fundamental principle on which Scripture authorization is explicit, namely, the use of inspired songs.

7. In view of uncertainty with respect to the use of other inspired songs, we should confine ourselves to the Book of Psalms.

Respectfully submitted,

John Murray
William Young

Rev. John Murray was a Scottish-born minister of the Orthodox Presbyterian Church, and Professor of Systematic Theology at Westminster Theological Seminary, Glenside, Pennsylvania, from 1937 to 1966. He died in 1975.

Rev. Dr. William Young, (b. 1918), is the retired minister of the East Greenwich, Rhode Island, congregation of the Presbyterian Reformed Church, and also served as Professor of Philosophy at the University of Rhode Island. He was a minister of the Orthodox Presbyterian Church until 1976.